FAMILY GARDEN

FAMILY

GARDEN

A practical guide to creating
a fun and safe family garden

LUCY PEEL

BARRON'S

First edition for the United States, Philippine Republic, Puerto Rico, and Canada
published by Barron's Educational Series, Inc., 2000.

Originally published in English by HarperCollins Publishers Ltd under the title
Collins Family Garden.

Text © Lucy Peel 1999.
Photographs © HarperCollins Publishers, 1999.

All inquiries should be addressed to:
Barron's Educational Series, Inc.
250 Wireless Boulevard
Hauppauge, NY 11788
http://www.barronseduc.com

International Standard Book No. 0-7641-0932-4
Library of Congress Catalog Card No. 99-31345
Library of Congress Cataloging-in-Publication Data
Peel, Lucy.
      Family garden/Lucy Peel.
      p.   cm.
      ISBN 0-7641-0932-4 (pbk.)
      1. Gardening. I. Title.
      SB453. P335   2000
      635–dc21   99-31345
                                   CIP

Color reproduction by Colourscan
Printed and bound by Rotolito, Italy

CONTENTS

planning a family garden

I t is amazing how often all a family's energy—
creative and physical—is reserved for the home,
while the garden is left as an afterthought. This is all
the more surprising when you consider the large
amount of time spent in the garden and how it can
enhance the quality of life and even health. Thinking
purely in monetary terms, your property is your
single greatest asset and it is foolish to neglect
the one thing—the garden—that can add so much
value to your home.

Before embarking on any work in the home or garden,
set aside time to work out exactly what you want
and draw up detailed lists and plans. No time spent in
planning is ever wasted. In fact, it can save a great deal
of money, effort, and frustration.

▶ starting from scratch

Below
An undeveloped
garden is a wonderful
opportunity to plan
your garden according
to your family's needs.

Many young families are attracted to new housing developments. They offer brand new houses with builders' guarantees, eliminating maintenance worries for a good few years.

They also offer the prospect of other young families to befriend, as well as conveniently placed facilities such as playgrounds, medical centers, and shops.

Planners and builders of new developments often concentrate all their attention on the houses rather than the gardens. These tend to be left as bare areas of either mud or grass. Although such spaces may look uninspiring, they offer a wonderful opportunity to create something entirely suited to your family's needs and personalities. Think of them as a blank canvas.

The first thing to do is to examine the soil. Once the hastily laid turf is peeled back, it usually reveals an unappealing mixture of rubble with the thinnest sprinkling of topsoil. So, if your home is less than five years old, the first thing to do, before you rush out and buy lots of plants, is to improve the soil. This may involve buying and working in more topsoil. You should incorporate as much organic matter as possible to make the soil nutritious and ready to take plants.

Next, look at the surroundings of the garden. There may be a busy road that you would like to screen off, or the garden may be overlooked by neighbors' windows, making privacy a priority. There may also be vast expanses of bare wall or fence that could be improved with a covering of climbers or painted in an attractive color.

working with what you have

If you have moved into an old house, there will probably be an established garden. This may have been beautifully kept or be a jungle, but either way, there are bound to be things you wish to change or adapt.

Consider the shape of the garden. If it is very square, you may wish to soften it by creating curved borders with flowing planting. Triangular or long narrow plots can also be transformed through design—for example, narrow sites can be enhanced by adding a diagonal feature (a flower bed, steps, or a path) and triangular sites can be changed by

creating a circular shape. Once your basic framework is in place, you will be ready to think of adding the plants that provide structures, color, perfume, flair, and flounce—the more transient stars of the garden.

As soon as you move in, walk around the garden and do a safety check. Remove any obvious hazards, such as poisonous plants (see page 97), barbed or rusty wire, and crumbling walls; cover ponds until you have time to consider safety measures. Mend or remove loose paving stones and trim back any dangerous branches and shrubs.

Do not be too hasty in removing established shrubs. You may not find a particular plant appealing, but it may provide a useful framework while other plants are becoming established. It is surprising how much better a shrub can look after pruning and with new planting around it. After all, if it does not grow on you, you can always take it out later.

Left
Think about the amount of time you have to spend for tending the garden. A garden with shaped lawns will require more work than one with straight edges, although you may think it is worth the extra effort.

Above

Think carefully before you remove any large plants and structures, such as trees and walls. Spend time getting to know your garden before making any major decisions.

Delay starting major work until you have been in the garden for a full year. You need to see a complete cycle of seasons to fully appreciate what is in your garden and how all its elements work together.

A delay will also give you the chance to watch how your children play in the garden. You may be surprised at the features that attract them. For example, an overgrown hedge that you had earmarked to be pulled up may prove to be the perfect site for a fort. You may have planned to buy them a climbing frame or metal-framed swing, only to discover that they are getting such enjoyment from climbing the trees that a swing from a sturdy branch, rope ladders, commando-style netting, and even a tree house, would be much more appreciated.

Throughout the year, make notes about the elements of the garden that give you the most pleasure and those that annoy you. In practice, you may find that the clothesline is too far from the house, that the outdoor lighting is insufficient, or that the position of outside faucets is impractical. On the other hand, you may discover that a flower border that seemed out of place is ideally positioned for maximum/minimum sunlight, frost risk, and perfect drainage. And what a wonderful excuse not to do any work in your first year!

▶assessing your family's needs

Every family is different, with its own unique mix of personalities and requirements. Before you start any work on a garden, have a good long think about your family; consider their likes and dislikes. Take time to examine your everyday domestic routines and your leisure time.

Right
Eating in the garden is one of life's pleasures. Think about whether you need to build a specific dining area or whether you will be happy simply placing a table on the lawn.

Below
Split levels within a garden create an illusion of space and provide distinct areas that appeal to all members of the family.

Are your home and garden always overflowing with your children and their friends? Do you enjoy entertaining? Are you an active person who cannot sit still for a minute, or are you always looking for the opportunity to relax with the newspaper and a cup of coffee in a quiet corner?

Have everyone make a wish list. You may get some highly impractical suggestions, but they will give you an idea of how each member of the family views the garden and how they would like to use it. You need to complete your list of family requirements before you can start planning their position in the garden.

Don't feel obliged to think in traditional terms: if nobody is bothered about a lawn, a vegetable patch, or a flower bed, then don't have one. You can always change your garden later when your family's requirements change.

▸practicalities

Above and below
Remember to plan storage space in your garden. Toys, equipment, and furniture all need to be placed somewhere when not in use.

Divide your list into headings. First come the practicalities, the mundane domestic needs of everyday life. These may be tedious to think about, but getting these details right will make the difference between an easy-to-run house and garden, and one full of little irritations—daily reminders that you could have done better if only you had given the project a little more thought.

storage

Every family needs storage space—for toys, bicycles, garden furniture, and equipment. This should be an adequate size for your requirements, easily accessible, and securely lockable. Sometimes you can use part of a garage, or there may be an area in your home that can be utilized; if not, a shed is the most sensible solution. Figure out how much space a shed will take up, and work this into your plan. Sheds are available in all sizes, including small lean-to designs, so there is bound to be one to suit your garden and budget.

garbage

Space for garbage cans is important. They should not be too far from the kitchen, yet you will also want easy access to the front gate for garbage collection. The area should be lit and you should also consider whether you need to build an enclosure to protect against vermin and pets. You may also want to think about ways to disguise the cans, such as fencing, so allow space for this, too.

clothesline

If you like to line dry your washing, then the clothesline should be easily accessible. The clothesline should not be too far away from the house, in case you need to make a rescue dash if it starts to rain. Think about what sort of drying set-up you prefer. There is a wide choice of dryers, including rotary lines (choose those set in sockets so they can be removed) and retractable lines. Consider safety, allow plenty of room for washing to flap without getting tangled in nearby plants, and remember that whatever you choose will need space and will affect your view of the garden.

Above
Careful planning of your front garden will make life much easier. Allow enough space for cars and bicycles, and a covered walkway can be useful in bad weather. Use low-maintenance plants and think about not having a lawn if you want an easier life.

kitchen garden

A kitchen and herb garden should be close to the kitchen, otherwise visiting it will become a chore rather than a pleasure. You will need easy access to water in the form of a hose extension or water hook-up, as well as to the compost heap and greenhouse.

car parking

Most families have at least one car, if not two, so a driveway, carport, garage, and parking space must be considered. Many homes already have a garage and a driveway, so their position will be fixed. However, their relationship to the rest of the garden can be altered by planting. For example, the walls of an ugly carport can be made to disappear behind a wall of shrubs. Climbers can be planted to scramble up the walls and cascade over the roof, and the edges of the driveway can be softened by spreading plants.

lighting

You will need different types of lighting for different purposes (see page 70). Convenience and safety are important, but remember that well-planned lighting can also transform a terrace and highlight unusual garden features.

maintenance

How much time do you have to spend on gardening? This is a very important question. Be realistic: there is absolutely no point in persuading yourself that you can easily look after huge borders of herbaceous plants when, in fact, you would be hard-pressed to prune a few shrubs and cut the grass.

▶leisure time

Onto the interesting part—planning your leisure time in the garden. Start by listing the fun things you plan to do, or dream of doing, in the garden.

eating outside

Everyone enjoys eating outside, so building or adapting a terrace or patio should be at the top of the leisure list. At the same time, you could consider a permanent, built-in barbecue, which can double as an outdoor fireplace and prolong your time spent outdoors.

playing

For children, playing takes precedence over everything else, so most children's wish lists will include every imaginable play structure, piece of equipment, or toy. Decide what is most suitable for your children, as well as what will fit in the garden: bear in mind that, as the children grow, you may want to adapt or modify their play space.

Right
You may choose to include a patio area for eating outside or for somewhere to sit and read the newspaper.

Left
Water is popular for many people, and depending on the age of your children, you may want to add a water feature. A shallow pond lined with pebbles is a more attractive option than one lined with plastic, and it doesn't have to cost a fortune.

lounging

For pure relaxation, all that is needed is a comfortable chair or hammock, and some peace and quiet. If you have space, incorporate other features, such as a summerhouse, a gazebo, or an arbor.

water features

Water safety is the main concern when planning a water feature. If you have young children, a pond may be out of the question, but there are several safe options to consider (see page 44).

attracting wildlife

If your garden is full of insect, animal, and bird life, it will not only be a more interesting place for your family, but a healthier, more balanced environment in which pests are gobbled up rather than killed by chemicals, and where plants thrive with the help of pollinating insects. So leave some wild corners and plant plenty of insect-attracting and berry-bearing shrubs that are attractive to insects and birds alike.

decorative features

These can elevate a garden out of the ordinary. Pergolas and arbors wreathed in plants convey a soft romantic touch, while an urn, statue, or other ornamental feature can add a wonderful element of surprise.

children's garden

You could set aside a piece of the garden for your children to call their own (see page 88) or plant trees to commemorate special events, such as births and anniversaries. Children will quickly come to love their tree, and you can keep a record of the tree's and your child's progress with yearly photographs and a height chart.

be extravagant!

Family gardens are the ideal place to indulge your imagination with lighthearted, playful features that reflect the personality of your family. Include a few oddities such as a sundial clock, or sink bricks with the hours painted on them into the ground in a circle and position them so that when your child stands in the center of the circle, his or her shadow falls across the correct hour.

You could include something to appeal to adults and older children, such as a giant chess and checkers board made with dark- and light-colored pavers. Hopscotch designs also lend themselves to this idea. Most gardens are too small for a full-size croquet lawn, but a modified version is possible. You could also set aside an area for badminton or softball, or construct a sandbox.

Above
This incredible sundial is situated on a small lawn of thyme and surrounded by clusters of pebbles. It is a stunning piece of sculpture and would be a talking point in any garden.

▶making a plan

Sketch a rough-scaled plan of the house and garden on a large sheet of graph paper. Start with the house and any outbuildings, and mark downstairs windows and doors. Add boundaries, such as hedges, fences, and walls, and all trees, shrubs, and beds that you want to keep. Terraces and paved areas, steps, paths, and ponds are all vital, as are changes in ground level. Consider the canopies of overhanging trees and mark good views or features with stars. Indicate north, the direction of prevailing wind, and the path that the sun takes over the garden during the day. Label very shady, very sunny, very wet, or very dry areas.

Once you have completed your rough sketch, measure your garden and all the permanent features and draw a clean, precise plan. This will help you make logical decisions such as where to place landscaping features. Your terrace or patio should not be situated where it gets raging wind, but where it receives the gentle warmth of the late afternoon sun. Your plan will help you satisfy both these requirements, as you will be able to tell at a glance the direction of the prevailing wind and where the sun shines at different times of the day. The plan will also help you avoid such disasters as erecting the children's swing and then finding out that their feet get tangled up in the branches of the apple tree as soon as they gain some height, or setting up compost bins at the end of a path that is too narrow for the wheelbarrow to get down.

All this may sound daunting, but it is actually very straightforward and is essential in getting to know your garden. It is an important exercise that helps you clarify ideas, work out which features and plants will suit the garden, and how to make it a truly user-friendly garden.

Always consider the garden in relation to the style, proportions, and scale of the house. There should be a smooth transition between the two—each must flow into the other. Think of the garden as an extension of the house, an extra room. Go around the house looking out of windows. Views into the garden are extremely important.

Allow the landscape, shape of the site, and surrounding areas to guide you. An urban landscape has as much to offer as rolling fields. Look for natural assets that can be highlighted or borrowed, such as a view— maybe this could be opened up and enhanced. Beautiful, mature trees and

Above
Curved lawns and abundant planting make this a stunning garden. It will, however, require daily maintenance to keep its shape.

Right
In contrast, this garden has a straight-edged lawn that will take less time to cut and the majority of plants are low-maintenance.

Above

Trees provide shade and privacy. They hardly need any maintenance and are a great addition to a family garden.

disguised or screened; and a strong, prevailing wind can be partially tamed by planting a barrier hedge to dissipate it. The most basic rule of all is to keep the initial design strong and simple. You can always add to it later.

When deciding what to plant, don't confine your thoughts to color, fragrance, and size. There is so much more that is important, such as shape, texture, movement, and sound. However, it is a very good idea to restrict the varieties of plants and colors. A border planted with bold clumps of flowers, maybe in a single color, looks much more striking than one containing a wide variety of plants in different colors, dotted here and there. Remember to plan your groups so that the smallest are at the front.

Trees are always a welcome addition, providing vertical interest, character, shade, and a place to play or sit. Many people don't want to plant trees because they may take a long time to grow, or because they plan to move on after a few years. But even a young tree will add enormous interest to your garden, and with many species, it is amazing how much growth can be put on in just three or four years.

Choose your tree carefully, avoiding thirsty or strong-growers such as willows (*Salix*) and poplars (*Populus*). These have a wide-ranging root system that may damage house foundations or hard surfaces such as paths and patios. Instead, look for trees that offer year-round interest in terms of shape, bark, blossom, berries, delicate new spring growth, and spectacular autumn colors. Flowering crab apples (*Malus*) are lovely, as are varieties of maple (*Acer*), mountain ash (*Sorbus*) and birch (*Betula*).

Try to picture how your garden will look as the seasons progress. You need to sustain interest throughout the year, so note when individual plants will look their best for flower, fruit, or foliage, and situate them so that they can be enjoyed from your main vantage points. Obviously, your soil type may

attractive neighboring buildings or walls can also be valuable features, so make the most of them.

Some features of the site cannot be altered without great expense, for example, if the ground is naturally very hilly. If this is the case, make these level changes work for you by creating an intriguing series of terraces linked by winding paths or steps. Each level can be different in character and the children can have their very own terrace for playhouses, swings, and climbing frames. Such gardens have a wonderful feeling of movement and space to them, with each terrace offering new delights to entice you into further exploration.

While some drawbacks may not be totally overcome, they can be alleviated in many ways. Shade can be reduced by judicious pruning; eyesores, such as oil tanks, can be

rule out certain plants, so if you are desperate to include them, plant them in containers.

Don't forget safety aspects (see page 97) and avoid plants that are poisonous, have irritating sap, or are dangerously thorny.

Finally, remember that children do not stay little forever, and as they grow, they will change their ways of using the garden. Instead of wanting a climbing frame, they may eventually prefer a secluded, scented arbor where they can talk with friends or read in privacy.

Be patient. If you have always yearned for a pond and are not able to have one while the children are very young, they will soon be old enough for water to be safe. If you adore delicate flowers and enormous herbaceous beds, there will be plenty of time to get these established once the children demand less of your time and have stopped throwing around footballs.

Above
A large flower bed in the center of a lawn can look great, but will require regular maintenance and may suffer after several games of football!

Right
If you have space, consider dividing your garden into an area for children to play, and a quieter corner where you can escape from them.

surfaces and boundaries

Once you have decided your plan for the garden, the next stage is to think about surfaces and boundaries. Before you think about soft aspects of landscaping—a lawn and flower beds—decide if you are happy with your hard landscape—fences, walls, steps, terraces, decks, and pergolas. The hard landscaping is the all-important framework within which the beauty of trees, shrubs, and flowers are contained; therefore, you must get it right before you can begin gardening.

▶boundaries

Boundaries represent more than just a marking of territory; they are important for privacy and security. They keep unwelcome humans and animals out, as well as children in, and they should also be designed to improve the look of the garden.

Top
An arch can divide the garden, marking a change in usage.

Above
Using fences and hedges as dividers within the garden provides privacy and creates an illusion of space.

When deciding on a design and materials, bear in mind the period and style of your house, as well as the materials with which it is built. The boundary should be in keeping with the house and blend with the rest of your design.

hedges

A living boundary in the form of a well-tended hedge is not only an asset to a house but to the local wildlife. A hedge also serves as a great barrier for wind and noise. The most suitable style of boundary hedge depends on the design and surroundings of the house. For example, a very formal clipped hedge would not suit a country home surrounded by fields, while a mixed country hedge would look rather strange outside an urban town house.

Other things to consider when planting a hedge are height and spread and its speed of growth, as this will determine how often you need to cut it. Choose hedging plants that will do well in your particular type of soil. Look around at neighboring gardens to see which plants looks healthy and happy; there is no point in trying to grow a lime-lover in acid soil. Also consider whether the plants will get enough light as they are growing and whether the ground is too dry. All these factors will determine how quickly the hedge grows and how dense it will be when mature.

As far as wildlife is concerned, a good mixture of native evergreen and deciduous hedging shrubs will be the most popular for nesting birds, food, and shelter. However, many people prefer an evergreen hedge for year-round privacy. This kind of hedge makes a strong shape that noticeably defines the boundary. If security is a worry, whether it be keeping unwanted visitors out or children in, a few prickly, spiky shrubs such as holly, pyracantha, and berberis make very effective barriers.

Good alternatives to evergreens are deciduous trees that can withstand heavy pruning to maintain shrub size and retain their leaves in winter. Beech (*Fagus sylvatica*) and hornbeam (*Carpinus betulus*) are excellent examples. In the autumn, their leaves turn a warm golden-brown but do not blow away, hanging on until the new buds appear in spring.

The main disadvantages of hedges are the time they take to establish and their maintenance. Hedges are also wider than a wall or fence, so they need more space. They are, however, worth the effort. If you are worried about the need for a temporary

Above
Ivy and a stone mask add interest to this beautiful stone wall.

Right
A hedge reduces the space in this small city garden, and it provides privacy and greenery for very little effort. The topiary balls continue the theme.

Below
A plain concrete wall has been transformed using shells stuck on with more concrete.

barrier, you can put up a cheap fence and plant the hedge in front of it. When the hedge has reached the desired size, you can remove the fence.

walls

Nothing beats the look of a well-built brick or stone wall, especially one that has weathered naturally. Its warm, rich look makes it a thing of beauty in its own right, even before it is covered in climbers.

Walls can be built of brick, stone, concrete, or even large boulders piled on top of each other without mortar to make a dry stone wall. They make a sympathetic backdrop for climbers, and if south-facing, hold the sun's warmth, creating an ideal position for fruit trees, such as figs and pears.

Keep in mind that a properly constructed wall, even a very low one, is very expensive due to the cost of labor added to that of materials. Another disadvantage is the wind factor, as solid walls create an area of wind turbulence that can harm plants.

fences

A fence provides an instant solution to the boundary problem. There are numerous different types of fencing material, many of which are very cheap, and they are usually very easy to erect because most types come in prefabricated panels.

Among the cheaper types of fencing are larch or pine overlap, basket weave, or lath. If you want something more unusual, look for woven willow or hazel wattle hurdles, or bamboo fencing. These can be more expensive than other fencing materials because

Above
Add interest to a standard overlap fence with containers, climbing plants, and a decorative trellis.

Below
A wicker fence creates a relaxed country look and is a good backdrop to a climbing rose.

natural wattle fences are handmade by craftspeople and do not last more than five or six years. However, they are extremely attractive, look wonderfully rustic, and work especially well as a stopgap while hedges grow and become established.

These more open fences also work well as wind breaks because they allow enough wind to filter through to diminish its ferocity. To achieve the same effect with a solid fence, attach trellis to the top and cover with a mass of climbers.

Open fences, such as split rail and picket fences, have a great deal of charm but do not provide much privacy, shelter, or security, so use this type of fencing sparingly.

If you have spare soil on site from excavations for ponds or level changes, try something completely different and erect a Cornish fence. This looks spectacular, yet is

very easy to erect. It consists of a wall of earth about 2 feet (60 cm) wide by 3 feet (90 cm) high contained between two hazel wattle hurdles. The hurdles are lined with marine ply for strength and durability. Once it is all in place, the earth is made firm and planted.

railings

Cast iron railings, often set on top of low walls, were very popular garden accoutrements in the eighteenth and nineteenth centuries, especially in the fashionable areas of cities. Today, it is possible to buy modern cast iron railings. They are not as heavy as the originals, but they are just as ornamental and add a welcome, classic, finishing touch to a more formal house and garden setting.

▶dividers within the garden

Hedges, walls, and fences also have a role within the garden. They can be used to define and protect a particular area, such as a kitchen garden, or to create interest, variety, and structure in your garden layout.

Below
Gates and fencing can be features in their own right. This gate leads the way to a small, secluded garden–ideal for adults seeking a hiding place!

An open garden can be made more intimate by a series of hedges planted to create different garden rooms, corridors, and walkways. By dividing a garden in this way, it can be made to seem much more extensive, and if it is planned properly with clearly defined paths, visitors will find themselves drawn to walk around the garden, exploring each twist and turn.

Informal low-growing hedges, such as germander and potentilla, work extremely well as internal dividers where the density of the hedge is not a major consideration.

Trellis, especially the decorative types with concave or convex tops and elegant dividing posts topped with finials, looks extremely smart when used to divide different areas of a garden. It looks good enough to use on its own, but when entwined with jasmine, climbing rose, or passion flower, looks even more spectacular.

gates

Gates are a feature in their own right. They can be plain and functional, or they can be decorative focal points. Whether you prefer ornate or plain gates, they should match both the house and the boundary in style, or they will look completely out of place. A modern, cast iron gate looks totally wrong set in a beautiful, old, stone wall, just as an elaborate Victorian gate does not work in a contemporary setting.

Besides self-closing, child-proof catches, it is well worth fitting rising buttress hinges on any external gates. The advantage of these is that they always swing shut, so children are less able to wander and burglars will not be alerted to an apparently empty house.

▶driveways and paths

Below
Crazy paving looks
attractive in a country
garden, especially if
made from stone or
natural-colored pavers.

Paths and driveways are vital elements in the design process because they not only link the house with the outside world, but, in the case of paths, they link different areas within the garden.

The shape you decide on for your paths and driveway has as much an effect on the impression they create as the materials with which they are surfaced. A straight front path and driveway create a feeling of formality and purpose and are usually best suited to small front gardens. Curves and undulating shapes look more natural and create a sense of movement and freedom, tempting visitors to explore, especially if your front garden is large, with the house set well back.

The overall shape of your plot and where the house stands within it will determine whether you choose straight lines or curves. A straight driveway and path may seem a little too ordered, but work extremely well with either a very modern house, or, at the opposite end of the scale, an old, grand house. A curved, or even circular driveway, with a curved path to the front entrance, looks at one with most country houses.

While practicality is obviously important, it is also vital to choose surface materials that look good and are in keeping with the style of the house, garden, and boundaries. All these considerations apply to paths around and through the back garden. A garden design is like a jigsaw puzzle in which no one element can ever be viewed in isolation and each part must fit together to make the whole picture.

driveways

Most visitors approach the house via the driveway, so it is vital to give this area thought when planning. After all, first impressions are important and so it is not enough just to choose the most functional shape and surface material.

Because the two are adjoined, the color of the house should be a guide to the ideal color of the driveway. A slightly deeper shade of the same color looks best. If you try to match color and shade exactly, the result may look somewhat monotonous.

Above
Covering the driveway with climbing plants softens the appearance of the area and looks welcoming.

Right
It is a good idea to add a path in an area that you frequently use.

paths

Paths can serve several functions in a garden. If you have a path leading to your front door instead of a driveway, think about the impression it creates on visitors. Paths also exist to link or divide different parts of the garden.

Obviously, the quickest route between any two points is a straight line, but a straight path will not necessarily do your garden justice. If a path is allowed to meander, with plenty of curves and little surprises along the way, such as a shady arbor with a bench to sit on or an interesting focal point to draw the walker on, it will help transform your garden into a place of magic and mystery.

Use planting to create paths with different atmospheres. For example, trees and shrubs can be planted alongside the paths to create a tunnel or allée effect. To make this even more dramatic, plan the tunnel so that it emerges into a bright, open area of the garden. The contrast will be striking.

You can make an entirely different tunnel effect by erecting a pergola or a series of arches planted with fragrant climbers. Enhance the romantic effect by placing an urn mounted on a plinth, a piece of sculpture, or an attractive container at the end as a focal point.

There are also numerous tricks you can employ to fool the eye into thinking that the path or garden is longer than it is. Other tricks can be utilized to change the shape of the plot altogether.

A particularly effective illusion is to lay the path so that it gradually gets narrower and narrower as it progresses. This makes it seem longer than it actually is. Alternatively, design a mysterious path that disappears behind a dense shrub or hedge. You may have nothing behind this other than a garden shed, but it will create the impression that there is a whole new area of the garden just out of sight.

If your garden is noticeably oblong or square, you can make use of a path to alter the visual perception of the shape. Simply lay the path so that it runs in a semicircle around the edge of the garden, creating a circular area of grass or hard surface in the center. This draws attention away from the hard boundary lines.

▶ surface materials

Paths and driveways must be practical as well as attractive. They must be wide enough for comfort and they must be constructed of materials that look good, fit in with the design of the house and garden, and are long-lasting and safe.

Below
Bricks are inexpensive and easy to use. Because they are so small, you can make a patio area any shape you like.

To decide which materials work best for your needs and within your design, look at the garden as a whole, examine how the different elements visually hang together, and consider the needs of your family. For example, a gravel driveway always looks extremely smart and suits any style of house, but your children might like to ride their bicycles on the driveway and paths, or you might need to push a stroller along them. If this is the case, then it may be better to abandon the idea of gravel.

Safety is another element that must be considered. A slippery surface is an invitation for cuts and broken bones and must be avoided at all costs. Stone slabs and brick surfaces can be particularly slippery in wet or icy conditions.

The choice of surfaces for driveways and paths is enormous and today's options are far more attractive than the old standbys of concrete and asphalt. There are paving slabs, tiles, bricks, and cobbles, as well as precast pavers. Look for local materials: these are more likely to blend in with existing elements in your garden. Check with your supplier to ensure that your choice can withstand the weight of a car.

Paving materials look very different depending on how they are laid. Small units such as pavers and bricks are quite busy, and square paving slabs can look totally different if laid point on, resulting in a diamond as opposed to grid pattern. Combinations of two materials of different size and texture, such as brickwork and paving slabs, can work very well together.

Whichever material you decide on, the end result will only be as good as the foundations upon which it is laid. Like any building or gardening job, preparation is of the utmost importance. Be sure to lay your driveway and paths on a properly consolidated base with, if necessary, sand on top. Build in a very slight slope to allow water to run off and away from the house. If you neglect this, water will gather, eventually damaging the surface and posing a danger in freezing weather. Avoid trees within 16 feet (5 m) of paths or driveways if possible, because the shade may make the surfaces slippery and the movement of roots may lead to uneven or sunken surfaces.

concrete

The main advantage of concrete is that it is cheap and easy to lay. It is also long-lasting and does not require much maintenance. Concrete is an extremely flexible material and can be bought as slabs, poured into molds to make shapes, or directly laid on a solid base and then finished either by smoothing or by imprinting to create any number of patterns. It can also be color tinted in numerous shades.

The harsh look of a large expanse of concrete can be considerably lessened by combining it with large pebbles, brickwork, or cobbles. These provide a visual distraction and break up the monotony. If you already have a concrete driveway or path and want to liven it up, then dig up sections—breaking up the concrete with a pickaxe or drill—fill with concrete, and inset any of the above materials. Keep your design simple, and, if in doubt about your abilities, call in a professional.

stone and paving slabs

Original, stone slabs always look extremely handsome, with their feeling of solidity and patina of age. Reclamation yards usually have good stocks, but they are generally expensive. A cheaper but equally attractive alternative is reconstituted stone slabs. These are man-made from precast concrete and aggregates. There is a huge range of these slabs available, and they are so realistic that it is virtually impossible to distinguish them from stone. Like real

Left
This path is made by pressing colored stones and pebbles into wet concrete. You could do this for a whole path or just in a few places to add interest.

Left
Alternating colors can make ordinary pavers look more interesting.

stone, they also age, improving with time and exposure to the elements until they become pleasantly mellow.

cobbles and precast setts

Cobbles and setts look wonderfully natural and are extremely hard-wearing, although cobbles are not very comfortable to walk on for long distances. Original cobbles can be difficult to obtain and laying them is a job for a professional. If it is not expertly done, individual cobbles can loosen and be difficult to reset.

Another option that looks just as good as a cobbled pathway is precast setts. This is a relatively new process that uses variously colored concrete or clay in a mold to produce a surface indistinguishable from the real thing. The end result is very tough, and the wide choice of tints allows you to find just the right shade to suit your house and its surroundings.

Above
This path has been made by pressing cobbles into the soil and allowing the grass to grow around them.

tiles, brickwork, and pavers

The patterning in bricks and pavers does not come from the material itself, but from the pattern of laying. Among the most common patterns are herringbone, running bond, and basket weave. Tiled paths work very well in an urban setting, particularly on the path leading to the front door. They are probably not suitable elsewhere in the garden, where they are liable to crack and become dangerously slippery with heavy use and exposure to planting. Slipperiness can also be a problem with bricks and some pavers, although a thorough cleaning with a high-pressure jet or a scrub with a stiff brush and soapy water will help keep the problem in check. Avoid special moss and algae treatments because they are unnecessarily harsh and eventually take the surface off the tiles or bricks.

When choosing tiles and bricks, check that they are frost-proof, otherwise they will start to flake and crumble. Pavers are very tough, being designed to withstand the weather and wear from cars and feet.

Clay and concrete tiles are available in every imaginable pattern and color, and while the choice of color for bricks and pavers is slightly more limited, it should be possible to find some to match your house without much difficulty.

gravel, crushed stones, and chippings

Gravel, crushed stone, and chippings are stone products. They are relatively cheap and can transform the look of a garden. They come in a variety of colors, which makes them excellent for matching with masonry or paint; washed or pea stones or chippings also lighten up a dark area—a huge advantage if your house faces north.

It is important to have stones or chippings properly laid. It is not enough to just dump out a truck-load and spread it around with a rake. It may look good for a little while, but rainwater will soon start to gather and in no time at all there will be weeds sprouting everywhere.

If you lay gravel on top of another surface, such as concrete or asphalt, first spray the whole area with hot bitumen or tar, sprinkle a single layer of stones or chippings, then roll. Once it has dried, you can add more loose material on top to the depth recommended by the manufacturers. This ensures that you will never reveal the subsurface even when a car turns and moves the top layer. Alternatively, it is possible to buy a self-binding gravel.

The downside of stones or chippings is that it is difficult to ride a bicycle on them or push a stroller or wheelbarrow over them. Also, both can cause nasty cuts if fallen upon and chippings have a tendency to spread into the flower beds and house. If you are concerned about children hurting themselves, then choose either washed or pea stones, as these have no sharp edges.

The other problem is that local cats may decide to use your gravel as a giant litter box. Cats can be discouraged from small areas with strong-smelling substances such as crushed mothballs or cat pepper.

steps
and edges

Above
Large pieces of slate
make great steps.

Below
Railroad ties and gravel
make unusual and
stylish steps.

Many gardens have different levels to be connected, even if only from the patio to the lawn. Ramps may be necessary if the garden is used by the elderly or handicapped, but for most families, steps are the best and most practical solution. They can be extremely beautiful in construction and materials, with incidentals, such as pots or plants, completing the picture and making them a decorative feature in their own right.

It is important to get the correct proportion of rise (the height of each step), depth, and width of the step. Aim for shallow steps, with a minimum rise of 4 inches (10 cm) and a minimum depth of the treads of 12 inches (30 cm). Make sure the steps are even and solid when finished, with the slightest tilt for water drainage.

The material that you choose for your steps should depend on the style of the house and garden and should tie in with other materials used in the construction of the garden. They can be built from any of the materials listed for paths and driveways, plus railroad ties and preservative-treated logs or lumber.

Steps that lead down from a terrace should be constructed of the same materials in order to look at one with it. Proportion is an important consideration. For example, a narrow flight of steps leading up to a broad terrace would look odd, whereas a wide sweeping flight of steps would look perfect.

design

When positioning your steps, it is important to consider their primary purpose. Are they simply fulfilling a practical need, for example, connecting the patio to the lawn, or are they to play a more decorative role in your garden? Whatever you decide influences their position. If they are mainly decorative, you may decide to follow the natural contours of the land so that they twist and turn. If they are purely functional, their position is more restricted.

The geography of the site also has a bearing on the most suitable shape for a flight of steps. In a steep, craggy, seaside setting, the steps may have to wind around rocky outcrops, while straight, wide, shallow steps can easily be accommodated in a garden set in gentle rolling countryside.

formal or informal?

The style of your house and garden should also determine the style of your steps. In a formal garden, elegant, curved, stone or brick steps, flanked by uniform pots filled with clipped box or bay, look very stylish.

Certain materials lend themselves to particular settings. Stone paving slabs are completely appropriate in a formal garden, while informal or contemporary gardens allow for much more experimentation. Old railroad ties, for example, are sturdy and cheap and make excellent steps, especially if combined with gravel as an infill. Preservative-treated logs are also suitable and look perfect in a wild or woodland setting. Wood becomes slippery when wet, but a sheet of chicken wire securely nailed over the logs or ties will solve this problem.

edgings

An edging is needed to finish off and retain steps and paths. It may be nothing more than planks of wood laid on their sides, or you can choose from a huge range of ready-made edgings that make the job easier and look smart.

For a purely functional area that is tucked away in a corner, such as a kitchen garden, plastic or aluminum strips or concrete edging are efficient but unattractive. A more pleasing alternative is to use bricks placed diagonally on end. These are decorative, easy to lay, and look equally at home in rambling country gardens or in more formal settings. For a more natural look, particularly suited to woodland gardens, use edgings of treated logs or large stones. Shells can fulfill the same function in seaside gardens, but can be easily damaged.

To add an historical feel to your garden, you might choose drawn wire edging or, if you need something more substantial, rope-top, fluted, or scalloped Victorian-style edging tiles. These more expensive edging materials are made in either terracotta or concrete and are available with little posts and finials for the corners.

If securely and carefully laid, all these edgings will enhance the look of your garden by helping to define different areas and by preventing gravel, earth, and stones from spreading where they are not wanted, making mowing infinitely easier.

▶patios, decks, porches and balconies

No garden is complete without some-where to sit, preferably a space large enough to set up a table and chairs for alfresco meals. If you place a table and chairs on grass, it cuts down the time you can use them because the grass will be dewy in the morning, and will get damp and cold in the evening. Chair and table legs sink into damp earth; you will have to move them every time you mow, and in time, the grass beneath them will become muddy and compacted. The obvious solution is to build a hard-surfaced area that can be used all year round.

Below
The design of this garden uses different surfaces to emphasize the various areas and their uses. The dining area is a patio and there is a grass play area for children.

In cities, where space is at a premium and gardens are small, paving over the whole garden to create a patio (originally mean-ing a paved, walled garden) may be the answer. However, if your garden is larger, you may be able to set part of it aside to build a separate patio or deck.

patios

A patio is usually the hard-surfaced area immediately adjacent to the house, though you could place it elsewhere. You can inte-grate the patio with the rest of the garden by surfacing it with the same materials that are used elsewhere on driveways or paths. Whatever you use should tie in with the materials of the house, especially since your patio will be used primarily as an outdoor room. Additional continuity can be achieved through harmonious planting.

Whatever you build must be large enough to accommodate a table and chairs and for people to move around behind the chairs if desired. You may also want to include enough space for containers and possibly one or two garden lounges and an umbrella. You could also consider space for a sandpit or barbecue.

Be sure to include some herbs in your planting plan. They not only look attrac-tive, but scent the air and are useful in the kitchen. Most herbs thrive in hot, dry con-ditions and cope well with neglect, so they are fine in containers, even if you occasion-ally forget to water them. Fragrant climbers planted to scramble up the walls of the house help prevent the patio from looking stark, and a simple water feature adds extra ambience (see page 44).

decks

Decks have become extremely popular in recent years. They are built of wood and can be erected anywhere in the garden or as a patio immediately adjacent to the house, providing a link from the inside of the house to the garden.

Wood is a lovely, warm material that, if properly treated, wears well. It requires minimal maintenance, but can be slippery when wet if not treated with a nonslip coating. Splinters can also be a problem, so use timber that is planed smooth for decked surfaces.

Decks offer versatility and are therefore particularly useful in steep, sloping gardens, or where there are a large number of trees, because it is very easy to build the deck around them. Since timber is such a natural material, you should have an informal plan for planting around the deck, creating the impression that the deck has somehow grown out of the garden. Bamboos work well, as do plants with large leaves and exotic foliage, such as varieties of *Rheum palmatum*, *Fatsia japonica*, and giant grasses.

porches

Porches are part of the structure of the house and should therefore be treated in a slightly different way from patios, terraces, and decks, even though these form a bridge between the house and garden.

A porch is usually roofed, so it makes a wonderful all-weather play area for children. It should be broad and shady, a place of retreat from the blazing summer sun and an all-purpose outdoors room where families can have meals, play, talk, and even do homework. You could prolong your use of this extra room by investing in an outdoor heater.

Lush planting, in pots or beds alongside the porch, creates a feeling of coolness, and a few pots of flowers that release their fragrance at night, such as lilies (*Lilium longiflorum*) or ornamental tobacco plants (*Nicotiana alata*), encourage guests to linger.

balconies

Balconies are a special attraction in urban settings with small gardens. If carefully planned, they provide a peaceful haven from the noise and bustle of the streets below, but it is vital to take safety factors into consideration. Before planning any balcony, have a qualified inspector ensure that it is structurally sound, with a damp-proof surface and the capacity to withstand the weight of containers filled with wet soil, plus any furniture.

Since surface space is limited, vertical planting is especially valuable. Trellis arches secured to the house walls provide an easy purchase for twining climbers and look decorative in winter when the foliage has died back.

Plant colorful clematis and perfumed white jasmine (*Jasminum polyphyllium*) and fill containers with scented flowers and shrubs. Since balconies are elevated, they tend to be exposed to the elements, so look for plants that cope well with drought and winds. Shrubs such as *daphne* and *skimmia* are suitable, as well as *pelargonium*, *nemesia*, and *helichrysum*. Pots of clipped lavender and rosemary look pretty and provide a nice fragrance.

Left
Decking can also be used as a pathway through a garden.

Right
This family has used decking across the whole garden, doing away with the need for a lawn. This cuts down on maintenance time in the garden, but keep in mind that decking can be very slippery when wet, so this might not be suitable for young children or the elderly.

▶grass and alternatives

Hard surfaces make for hard landings. Since children spend so much time falling down—whether from a rough tackle in football, a mistimed jump when skipping rope, or simply tripping over their own feet—a child-friendly surface is necessary.

Below

Looking after a lawn can be hard work, but it is ideal for children to play on. Choose a durable strain of grass if you don't want your lawn to turn into a mud bath.

grass

The most obvious surface is grass. It looks good, is a pleasure to sit on, and smells good when freshly cut.

Most families enjoy an area of grass to sit or play on, and the key to keeping a family lawn looking good is to choose a suitable grass mixture for your needs. Those including resilient rye grass are ideal for a durable lawn. Check with your local extension agency or a garden center for a recommended grass for your area. Don't mow the lawn too short, but set the blades higher than you would for a more manicured lawn so that the minimum finished length is ¾ to 1 inch (2 to 2.5 cm).

In heavily used areas, such as beneath a swing or climbing frame, lay rubber mesh with black rubber matting tiles on top. These are held in place with specially designed pins. The mesh spreads the load and ensures that the tiles do not damage the turf; as the grass grows up through the mesh and tiles, it completely hides them. The joy of this system is that it both protects the grass and allows you to mow whenever you please.

alternatives

If you live in a very wet climate, it may be better to choose an alternative surface, because grass takes quite a while to dry after rain and can all too easily deteriorate into a permanent patch of mud.

natural

Areas that get much use, such as the ground beneath a swing, can become so

compressed that it becomes as hard as concrete. In such places, a few bags of chipped bark, which is available from any garden center, should be laid as a mulch. It instantly creates a surface that blends with its surroundings and provides a very soft landing. Sand is also a good surface under swings and climbing frames. However, it is best avoided if you have pets, as they may decide to use it as a giant litter box.

man-made

Over the past few years, a number of man-made crash surfaces, previously only seen in public playgrounds, have appeared on the market. These consist mainly of treated cork or porous rubber matting and tiles, which come in every color of the rainbow.

They are excellent, safe surfaces with built-in bounce and are weatherproof and tough enough to cope with extremely hard wear. The downside is that they are relatively expensive and many should be laid by a professional qualified contractor. It does, however, last for years, and when the children have outgrown the area, it could then be used as an alternative area for outdoor dining.

Artificial turf has been around for many years and, although it is also fairly expensive, it is a good all-weather surface that has proved itself very durable. It is easy to maintain, needing only the occasional hose-down, and it is simple to lay. It provides a gentle landing, and will withstand much more wear-and-tear then real grass.

Above
Bark chippings have been used in playgrounds for years and they are now available in garden centers. When your children have outgrown their play area, use the chips in your flower beds to keep weeds at bay.

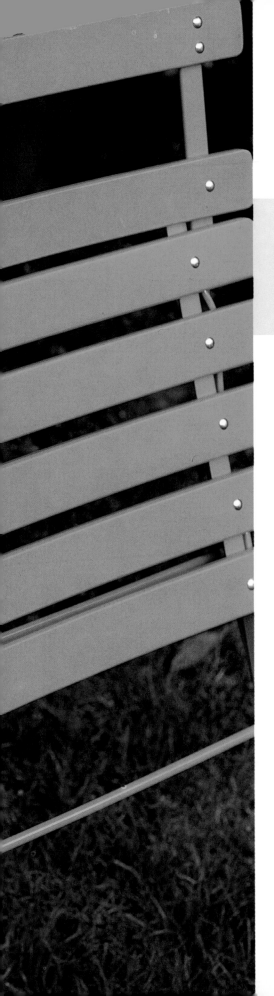

furniture and equipment

Furniture must do more than look good and suit the style of your house and garden. It must be comfortable, strong, and able to withstand daily family life. Few families have an unrestricted budget, and although you may prefer a quality piece that will last for years, it may be more practical to buy more temporary items. However, spend as much as you can manage on sturdy, safe, well-constructed furniture.

For practical purposes, it is important to consider maintenance and storage when choosing furniture. Does it stack or fold? Do you have somewhere to store it? Is it sturdy enough to be left exposed to the elements all year round? This chapter also looks at other features and equipment that you might like to include in your garden, such as water features and sheds.

▶chairs and tables

Above
Folding chairs are easy to store. This one has a hole in the back so that it can be hung out of the way.

Below
Solid wooden furniture is timeless and looks great in a garden. It will also last for years.

Visually, chairs and benches may be decorative enough to act as focal points, drawing the eye toward a particularly attractive spot. They should tempt you to sit down and rest, and to contemplate and enjoy the beauty of the garden. A warm, sheltered spot may be ideal, or, if you prefer, a refreshingly cool, shady corner.

wood

Solid wooden furniture is natural, very sturdy, and lasts a long time. There are many handsome designs available, both traditional and modern, in a wide variety of grades and finishes of timber.

Hard woods, if left to weather naturally, gradually develop a beautiful silvery patina. However, if you want to maintain its original color, an annual rub down with oil is all that is needed. Soft woods, pressure-treated with preservative and finished with a preservative stain, last well. Colored woodstains do not give long-term protection because they do not penetrate the wood deeply enough.

A practical choice for families with young children is a wooden picnic table with built-in benches. These work well in informal gardens and are extremely safe, especially if you have young children who are prone to tipping over chairs. There are scaled-down versions available that look charming placed outside a playhouse or in a children's garden.

plastic

Plastic chairs are unbeatable for comfort, as they are molded to the shape of the body. They are tough and able to withstand any weather. They need nothing more than the occasional wipe down and they are

stackable, thus reducing storage headaches. Yet while they may be practical, they are not usually very attractive. White soon becomes grubby and scuffed, so choose a dark color, such as green, and dress it up with attractive green and white striped seat cushions and a matching tablecloth to improve its appearance. Most plastic tables can be collapsed for winter and those that cannot be folded up usually come with protective covers. A table with a hole in the middle for an umbrella is useful.

Top
Deck chairs are favorites in the garden. They also look good indoors, especially if you have a wooden floor.

Above
Iron furniture is expensive but very durable. Add cushions from your indoor dining chairs or living room to make it more comfortable.

canvas
Canvas directors' chairs look extremely smart, are very comfortable, and are just the right height for dining. They also fold up for easy storage. However, the material should not get wet and it can be difficult to clean, so it is best to avoid very pale colors. Directors' chairs look good with solid wood, metal, or plastic tables.

metal
In recent years, wrought and cast iron garden furniture has undergone a tremendous revival and now there are many delicate, curly, or dramatic gothic designs on the market. Lightweight alternatives are cast aluminum or wirework furniture, which share the good looks of wrought and cast iron, although both will rust. Metal furniture is very elegant and, depending on its style, suits both formal period and minimalist town gardens. It can be left outside all year as a permanent garden feature, and its ornamentation provides a strong, moveable focal point. In general, however, metal is colder and less comfortable than wood.

stone, slate, and marble
Garden furniture made from these materials is grand enough to attract the eye, yet definitely not portable, so you should carefully consider its position. It is possible to buy a ready-made table, but these are expensive and it may be more fun and much cheaper to put one together from different pieces found in reclamation yards, for example, slips and hearths from old fireplaces. Some quarries and stonemasons also sell direct to the public. Stone weathers beautifully, growing silver or orange lichen in sunny spots and velvety moss in shady ones. A coat of natural yogurt or buttermilk will help speed up this process.

rustic seats and tables
Whether roughly hewn from solid logs, or made of twiggy larch poles, rustic seats and tables look homemade and eccentric. It is this quality, and the knowledge that they are originals, which makes them so attractive. Like wrought and cast iron furniture, a well-made piece makes an excellent focal point in a garden.

wicker
It is worth seeking out wicker and cane if you want to create a 1920s or 1930s look. These pieces are very comfortable and lightweight, and are only suitable for fine weather or an enclosed porch, but look just as good indoors or out, so they can be stored in the house during winter. A major advantage is that this type of furniture can still be purchased fairly cheaply, and although you may not be able to find complete sets, you can achieve a personalized and stylish look by mixing and matching.

Above

A wooden seat wrapped around a tree looks very stylish and blends well with garden surroundings. You can buy kits that fit around any tree.

café chairs

French café chairs, made of metal and wooden slats, are extremely light and fold flat. They are better suited for dining rather than lounging, as they are somewhat small and flimsy—qualities that make them the perfect choice for a balcony or small terrace. For a truly continental feel, look for matching, round, metal tables.

benches

Perfect for a sun-soaked terrace or secluded corner, there are endless varieties of benches available, from curvy metal and plain teak, to more stately styles. Old-fashioned barrow benches are perfect if you want to enjoy several corners of your garden, as they can be rolled along, following or avoiding the sun. Stone benches retain the heat, so they can be very pleasant to sit on, although if you linger too long, they may start to feel painfully hard.

Try to find a place in your garden where you can build an informal seat, such as in the retaining wall of a raised flower bed. Don't be afraid to experiment. For example, build a marine ply or brick frame, fill it three quarters full with rubble, finish the top quarter with topsoil, and then plant chamomile (*Chamaemelum nobile*) to create a living seat. You can sit on chamomile and it also releases a wonderful fragrance. Extremely popular during England in Elizabethan times, such seats were said to aid relaxation. You should also exploit any natural features in your garden, such as a grassy bank. If you need to cut down a tree, leave the stump as a little picnic table for the children.

Any garden with trees should have a tree seat. These can be smart-looking cast iron or delightfully rustic, made of wood. It is possible to buy kits, which are very easy to assemble and do not require any sawing or sanding. Simply varnish, stain, or paint and you have a beautiful and practical feature that everyone can enjoy.

A swing seat is an irresistible place for morning coffee or relaxing evening drinks. Simple swing seats can be made from a plank of wood and attached to a secure beam, branch, or the roof of a porch by strong chains or ropes. More elaborate, freestanding swings are also available, with metal frames, comfortable padded cushions, and waterproof canvas canopies.

recliners

The cheerful striped canvas of deck chairs has long conjured up images of outings to the beach. Unfortunately, deck chairs are also associated with jokes about people hopelessly struggling as they try to put them up, falling through worn canvas and fighting to get out of them. Yet modern deck chairs have come a long way since then, and while it is still possible to buy the traditional style, there are alternatives available that are simple to erect and have armrests for comfort and to help you get up. In short, they have become fashionable classics, and because they fold flat, they are an excellent choice if space is tight.

Metal, tube-framed lounges with foam-filled, removable, padded cushions are inexpensive and widely available. They are

Right

Traditional wood and canvas umbrellas are worth the extra investment because they are sturdy and can withstand years of family use. They also tend to be larger than metal-framed umbrellas, which means that more people will benefit from their shade.

very comfortable and are easily adjustable to recline at different angles, from upright to flat. The other great bonus is that they fold flat and are extremely light.

The king of recliners, steamer chairs get their name from the fact that they were first used on cruise liners, but their smart, sleek, and timeless design also looks at home in a family garden. They are extremely sturdy, usually made of solid teak with removable cushions, so they are an excellent long-term investment. The main drawback is that they are expensive.

The ultimate portable recliner is the hammock. No grown-up can resist the lure of a hammock on a hot summer day. Hammocks are also a great source of fun for all the family. It is now possible to buy free-standing hammocks, or those with a v-shaped frame holding one end while the other is attached to a tree. Canvas or woven material hammocks are preferable to string mesh, which can be quite uncomfortable unless made of pure cotton.

umbrellas and canopies

An umbrella or canopy is essential to protect your family from the sun. Wood and canvas umbrellas are reassuringly heavy, tend to be larger than metal and cloth umbrellas, and look luxurious as well as decorative. They are slightly more expensive than metal-framed umbrellas, but add such class to a garden that they are well worth the extra money.

There are various gazebo-style canopies that are useful for gardens without natural shade. These canopies are made mainly of waterproof cotton and galvanized steel tubing, so they are lightweight and can be easily collapsed for storage. Some are large enough to eat under, while others are just big enough to accommodate a few chairs. Canopies with mesh sides can be rolled up to allow cooling breezes to enter, or lowered if insects are a problem.

▶water features

The sound of running water is not only relaxing but extremely refreshing. The play of light on the surface of a pond, the flash of color and sparkle as sunlight catches a splash of spray from a fountain, all add an inimitable quality that can transform a garden from being merely pleasant to being spectacular.

Below
This millstone fountain set on a bed of cobbles is very safe for children; the water runs off the stone and never collects to any depth. It is also strong enough to withstand lots of climbing.

The Moors in Spain understood these qualities. In the Alhambra garden in Granada, there are numerous pools, fountains, and rills and the air is filled with the musical sound of water. Even if you don't have such grand plans, you can still use water to great effect.

ponds, pools, and rills

Still ponds, pools, and rills make peaceful places to sit beside and contemplate. The reflection of the sky, clouds, and trees in the water is hypnotic and tranquil, and the gentle rustle of reeds or grasses makes a pleasant, soothing sound.

Parents of very young children are understandably nervous of the dangers of water, and although a pond or rill can be made safe with metal grids, it may be wiser to think in terms of an alternative water feature such as a pebble pool or wall-mounted trickle fountain. However, for families with older children, a pond, pool, or rill should not be dangerous and provides hours of entertainment.

The most suitable type of pond or pool for a family garden is informal, with plants spilling over the edges and a natural-looking beach of pebbles. Gently sloping sides are appreciated by wildlife and paddling children (see page 83).

It is possible to buy a preformed rigid pool, but it is more fun to design your own pool, using heavy-duty butyl or PVC liner. Dig the hole to the depth and shape you desire, remove any sharp debris, lay a thick 2 inch (5 cm) layer of sand, spread out and smooth the liner, then fill with water. Next, hide the edges of the liner under a mixture of large stones and smaller pebbles, soil, and gravel, then plant the surroundings.

A pool will soon develop its own eco-system, with insects, snails, and frogs inhabiting it. When choosing the type and amount of fish, consider their ultimate size and whether they will be able to cope with winter. When you buy the fish, ask the salesperson to supply you with this information. Also remember that fish need to eat and that frog's eggs are a fish deli-cacy. So if you want frogs to breed, you will have to build a fish-proof enclosure in which the eggs can develop into tadpoles and subsequently frogs.

Oxygenating water plants are vital to the health of the water because they provide the oxygen necessary for survival. However, many water plants are extremely invasive, so vigilance is required to keep them under control.

Rills, or straight narrow channels, are particularly suited to formal gardens. A long rill might run along the middle of a paved area with a gazebo at one end and give pleasure to both grown-ups and chil-dren. Adults will appreciate its elegant symmetry and classicism, while children will enjoy the thrill of sailing boats and spotting fish.

miniature pools

Any sort of watertight container can be made into a freestanding or sunken minia-ture pool. Such small containers are more manageable in terms of safety; a grid can be fixed just below the surface of the water and the plants threaded through it, hiding it almost completely.

Above
This raised pond edged with logs has a small fountain made from terracotta plant pots. The logs make a nice seat, but you will need to watch young children when they are near the pond.

Above
This stylish rill is connected by small waterfalls coming from pieces of slate.

Right
A millstone pond is ideal for a small garden. Again, this is a safe water feature because the water does not collect to any depth.

As long as they are frost-proof, old wooden half-barrels, stone troughs, terra-cotta urns, and ceramic Chinese dragon jars all make excellent water features. Filled with irises, glyceria, and dwarf water lilies, they can look spectacular, and if the container is large, you could even consider adding fish.

fountains

If you want the sound of water but do not want to bother with plants, then a free-standing fountain may be the answer. These should not be placed alone on a lawn or terrace, but set amid a sea of ferns or other foliage where they will look extremely striking. The wide range of designs, from traditional Victorian to contemporary stone and terracotta fountains, means that it is easy to find the right one to suit you and the style of your garden.

Wall fountains are attractive features, which look as good in modern urban gardens as in formal period settings. Mounted on a wall or brick plinth, they mostly consist of an all-in-one unit made up of a decorative mask that spouts water into a bowl. The water is pumped back up to the fountain via a plastic tube by a small unit hidden within the mask.

It is also possible to buy the elements separately and fit them together as you desire. This allows you to alter the distance between the water spout and bowl, which will affect the sound—the further away the bowl is from the spout, the louder the sound of the water.

You can choose from a wide range of styles including fish, gargoyle, or animal head masks in terracotta, stone, lead, or even fiberglass, with the water spout coming out of the mask's mouth. Any sort of proportionately sized container can be used to capture the water. Shallow stone shells and half-barrels work well: for extra safety, fill the container to the top with pebbles. Even 2 inches (5cm) of water depth can be lethal to a small child.

The safest water features are bubble fountains. These consist of a container completely filled with large pebbles. Beneath the pebbles is a hidden pump and a reservoir of water, into which a plastic tube is placed. This is fed through the pebbles for water to bubble out. The tiny jet of water should be just strong enough to keep the pebbles glistening wet—a cooling treat for hot, little, bare feet. But do bear in mind that mischievous children may want to pick out all the pebbles and throw them around the garden.

decorative features

Above
Containers can be positioned on any spare piece of garden.

Water features are without a doubt decorative, yet any garden also benefits from the addition of a structural feature. A well-placed urn, an unusual sculpture, an attractive statue, or an interesting *objet trouvé* adds immeasurably to the character of your garden and an arbor, gazebo, or pergola always adds a touch of romance.

Above
Containers are very easy to plant and add interest to any garden, whatever its size. You could use pots from a garden center or just look around to see what you can find for something a little different.

containers

As previously emphasized, the design of the house and garden should guide all your decisions on the style, size, materials, and position of all your garden furnishings. After all, nothing looks more pretentious than an unpretentious home or modern condominium with a grand urn in the middle of the front lawn. The result is pompous and laughable rather than impressive, whereas an old wooden half-barrel or terracotta pot bursting with flowers would look smart and totally in keeping.

You can use containers to create focal points. Grow a brightly colored shrub in a container, then move it as it outgrows its pot to fill an awkward gap in a border. Containers also allow you to grow shrubs or perennials that would not normally take to your soil. Camellias and azaleas, for example, like an acid soil, so are normally out of the question in alkaline areas; but you can mix up an ericaceous compost, pot it up, and cheat nature.

Think laterally when choosing containers. The most unexpected articles can look great when planted up. For example, an old gallon olive oil can, tin tub, or watering can will take on a new life when filled with colorful flowers. If your home is near the sea, an old-holed dinghy bursting with nasturtiums looks colorful and adds character. Various sizes of clay drain pipes are especially useful as they add height to a grouping of pots.

There are so many terracotta and glazed pots available that as long as they are frost-proof, you can find one suitable for every style of garden. Colored pots allow you to reflect an overall color scheme that you may have chosen for hard landscaped structure and planting.

For a more formal or oriental feel, seek out ceramic dragon jars, which you could emphasize with color-coordinated planting. Wooden tubs are excellent for framing doorways or steps, or you could plant two tall sunflowers to stand at attention beside a bench or doorway.

You can group together containers of different shapes and sizes for the most dramatic effects. This not only makes watering easier but reduces evaporation. Placing containers on damp gravel also reduces water loss.

Old lead urns and planters have a lovely soft look and feel to them, but are classified

Top
This garden bench has had two large holes cut into it so that containers can be inserted, making an inexpensive bench look much more interesting.

Above
Group containers together for maximum impact. This way they are also easier to water; you won't need to walk around the garden with a watering can.

as antiques and therefore extremely expensive. Luckily, there are now many *faux* lead pieces on the market that look exactly like the real thing yet cost a fraction of the price, so no one is deprived of the pleasure of owning such a classic feature.

Urns and some of the largest terracotta containers have enough presence and grace to stand empty. However, if you decide that this looks too stark and you want some plants, keep your choice simple. Less is definitely more when it comes to planting an urn. Stick to one or two plants and colors. A busy mixture may look good in a tub but will detract from the stateliness of an urn.

For smaller gardens, window boxes, hanging baskets, and wall-mounted pots are invaluable. They provide the means to add an extra splash of color when all the growing space on the ground is full. Hanging baskets should overflow with their mass of foliage and flowers, tumbling down until the basket is completely obscured. Window boxes look best when they are positioned just below the level of the window, so that you can look down on the plants without any risk of them blocking out light. Wall pots, such as galvanized steel containers, look good even before you add the plants!

what to grow

Besides the obvious flowers and climbers, experiment with herbs, vegetables, fruit, and even small trees.

herbs
Herbs grow easily in pots. In fact, some herbs, such as mint, are best restrained to prevent their invasive habit. Parsley, sage, oregano, basil, and chives all grow well in hanging baskets, window boxes, and containers. Place a window box on your kitchen sill or fix a "rise-and-fall" hanging basket to a wall outside, and you will have freshly growing herbs immediately on hand. To flank a doorway or flight of steps, a pair of clipped bays looks very flattering.

vegetables
The most commonly grown containerized vegetable is the tomato; however, they also thrive in hanging baskets and window boxes, as do peppers, chillies, and miniature eggplants. Lettuces and cabbages are decorative enough to grace any window box. Mangetout, runner, and French beans planted in a pot and trained to scramble up a wall or teepee of bamboos look very pretty. Tripods or teepees pushed into pots also make excellent supports for squash, zucchini, and cucumber. Even potatoes and carrots can be grown in containers.

fruit
Strawberries are often grown in specially designed terracotta containers with holes in their sides, yet many types of fruit trees also thrive in large containers. Specially bred dwarf apple trees take up little space, and in spring they can be moved to a spot where everyone can enjoy their glorious blossom. Plums also do well in containers, and figs actually fruit better if their roots are contained. Miniature orange and lemon trees look delightful on a sunny terrace or balcony, but must be taken indoors at the first hint of frost.

▸buildings and structures

Even a small garden benefits from some sort of decorative structure, whether it be a tiny gazebo that doubles in winter as a storage room, or a pretty arch framing an entrance.

Below
This old chimney pot cost just a few dollars and adds lots of interest to this border.

Classical statues are generally more suited to formal gardens than family gardens, although clever positioning can vastly improve the appearance of a mass-produced statuette. For example, reconstituted stone or cement lions can look very dramatic if given a few coats of natural yogurt or liquid manure to speed up the aging process, and if concealed in the midst of a leafy border.

Not many people can make a piece of original sculpture that fits in a family garden; but you can transform found objects, such as an interestingly shaped piece of driftwood, stone, or shell, into pieces of art by placing them on a homemade brick or sawn timber plinth, chimney pot, or overturned length of clay pipe.

Choose your setting carefully. The intersection of two pathways, the end of a series of arches, or a backdrop of a dark, dense hedge will show off your chosen object to the fullest.

Old garden tools, such as a rusted roller or old-fashioned wheelbarrow make excellent decorative features. The rule is that nothing must *look* contrived, however contrived it may actually be.

Sundials are pretty features that children adore. As your children follow the changing shadows on the dial, they will not only chart the progress of the sun across the sky, but learn to tell the time.

An effective way to liven up a border is to add vertical interest with obelisks made either of trellis or metalwork. It is fairly simple to make an obelisk from four wooden posts and pieces of trellis, topped with a finial; however, metal ones are also available in flat packs, with pieces that

Above
Even a piece of driftwood found on a beach makes an interesting feature in the garden.

Above
Old gardening objects such as this watering can look good tucked into a flower bed. An old roller or a stack of broken pots would also make attractive focal points.

easily slot together. Train some colorful climbers up your obelisk and you have a smart focal point.

Transform a simple seat into a place of beauty and tranquility by surrounding it with an arbor. Or, provide welcome shade from the sun by erecting a beamed wooden arbor over a patio and using it as an attractive support on which to train scented climbers and vines. Construct a pergola and smother it with roses and honeysuckle.

A piece of topiary is always eye-catching. Experiment with simple shapes, such as balls and domes, before attempting anything more complicated. It is easy to clip a pyramid shape with the help of a frame or to create a piece of false topiary. Any dense shrub, such as holly, yew, box, *riburnum*, or sweet bay *lonicera*, is ideal to work with.

Lath houses and gazebos are more serious structures, yet they do not need to be overly expensive. Carefully placed, painted, or color-stained and clothed with clematis and jasmine, the humblest prefabricated building becomes irresistibly romantic.

These are features that the entire family can use. For adults, a gazebo or lath house makes a perfect spot for relaxing with morning coffee or an evening drink, and children will treat it as an exotic playhouse.

To add more interest to a backyard corner for children, create natural climbing structures that help children use their imagination. You can arrange large, old logs from trees that have fallen down or have been cut down. If you don't have any available on your property, contact your city tree department or a commercial tree company for procuring logs. Have an artistic family member or friend carve them into alligators or dragons to make them truly original and interesting for children.

"Jumping stumps" can also be placed in a back area of the garden. They are basic structures and children will thoroughly enjoy them. Simply place about a half dozen tree stumps (flat, cut side up) about 1 to 2 feet (30 to 60 cm) apart from each other. Children will delight in skipping and jumping from one to the other.

▸tools and storage

A beautiful garden needs to be maintained, and to do this all sorts of equipment is required, from spades to hedge cutters. As when buying plants, the key to success is to buy the best. Initially, this may seem extravagant, but it will pay in the long run, because good quality tools, if well maintained, will last many years.

Below
A little paint can make a boring garden shed more interesting, as can a couple of wall-mounted pots.

With electrical equipment, safety is paramount. Thick gloves, goggles, and boots must be worn, and the tools should never be used in damp conditions. Use electric equipment that is double-insulated and UL-approved.

Always follow instructions carefully with regard to the correct way to hold a tool with the lead looped out of the way. When cutting hedges or trimming trees, use a stable ladder and make sure someone holds it steady. Never lean too far forward, tempting though it may be, to reach that last untrimmed area.

hedge trimmers

There are three types of hedge trimmers: electric, gasoline-powered, and rechargeable. Electric hedge trimmers are the cheapest, they are light, and they give good results, though the cord can be a nuisance. Gasoline-powered hedge trimmers produce excellent results, and it is a pleasure not to have to worry about trailing cables. On the other hand, they are heavy, noisy, and expensive. Rechargeable trimmers are the safest, but they have limited power and are time-consuming to recharge.

chainsaws

Never attempt to use a chainsaw, whether gasoline-powered or electric, without basic safety training. Like hedge trimmers, electric chainsaws are quieter and lighter than gasoline-powered machines, but they do not have as much power, so are not suitable for large gardens with numerous trees.

mowers

Any garden with grass requires a mower, and the size and type you choose will depend on the area that needs cutting. There is an enormous variety, with a mower available for every type of lawn.

Hand push-reel or power reel mowers are perfect for small lawns. They will also, along with edgers, make light work of awk-

Right
This small gazebo
structure makes an
attractive shed, but be
sure to keep chemicals
and sharp tools locked
away from children.

Powered shearers and weeders take a great deal of the effort out of tedious, back-breaking jobs. However, power weeders are not as accurate and thorough as their manual equivalent, and shearers are only really suitable for small lawns.

automatic watering systems

Any busy gardener (and that must include anyone with a family) will find an automatic watering system a wonderful timesaver. There are a number of different systems from which to choose, and they can be used for balconies, patios with containers, vegetable gardens, and paved gardens.

During hot weather, pots need to be watered once a day and hanging baskets more frequently. This is very time-consuming, and is one of those chores that tends to be forgotten. Unfortunately, such forgetfulness is fatal to the thirsty plants, which, in very hot weather, will wilt away in a matter of hours.

Although an automatic system may be expensive to install, ultimately it will save you money by ensuring that a number of plants are not wiped out at one time simply because you are busy and have forgotten to water them.

The simplest type of automatic watering system involves little more than an ordinary sprinkler controlled by a computerized timer. In areas where water shortages occur, sprinklers may be banned during certain months.

The alternatives are underground sprinklers, trickle, or drip feed systems. Underground sprinkler systems consist of PVC pipes, which feed a network of hoses, watering heads, and sprinklers. Installing such a system is complicated and should be left to a specialist company. Trickle or drip systems are excellent for terraces and balconies and, in the open garden, for borders or vegetable gardens. They are normally fitted with a timer to avoid wastage and with a removable filter for cleaning.

ward corners, slopes, and edges, so for big gardens they are wonderful additions to the lawn task force. Rotary mowers are the best tool for tackling long grass and rough ground, but do not give the fine, sharp cut of reel or cylinder mowers. These mowers produce either a utility cut or quality trim suitable for a luxury lawn and are best for achieving a striped finish.

If you have a large lawned area, then a gasoline-powered riding mower will save you hours of time. But if you have any sharp bends or corners, you will need a trimmer or hand-push mower to finish off.

shredders, shearers, and weeders

Every garden produces its share of prunings that are too woody for the compost bin. A shredder reduces this material, saving you the effort and waste of burning it or removing it from your property, and helps to improve your compost.

Above
Climbers, trees, and a garden bench help to disguise this shed.

practical buildings

Every gardener needs tools and equipment, such as pots, bags of compost, fertilizers, and so on, as well as barbecues, garden chairs, patio umbrellas, and play equipment. It follows that every gardener needs a place to keep all of this clutter. Any gardener interested in growing food will also find a greenhouse and potting shed indispensable.

sheds and storage

If your garden is large enough, a garden shed is more than a luxury, it is a necessity. Ideally, it should be large enough to be a workshop and a place to pot plants, with with enough space left to store your tools, children's toys, and garden furniture.

When choosing a shed, be sure that it is solidly constructed and that the timber has been treated to withstand the weather—pressure-treated timber is preferable to dipped timber. Check that the windows and doors open smoothly, that the roof is strong, and that it has gutters. The other important point is the floor, which will need a firm, flat foundation, such as paving or concrete.

Those with small gardens have more of a problem. It may be possible to set aside part of a garage for gardening supplies, and there is always the under-the-stairs storage area. However, this area is often reserved for coats and golf clubs and, being in the house, is far from ideal. One solution is to build or buy benches with lift-up lids for the patio, to provide seating as well as storage space. There are also storage units and lean-to sheds just big enough for tools. These are usually made from pre-painted steel or fiberglass.

greenhouses

Anyone with a family will be aware of all the additives in food, and if they have the space, will be anxious to grow their own fruit and vegetables. A greenhouse provides the best place for germinating your seeds.

There are two basic types of frame: wood and aluminum. Wood looks more traditional and rustic and so suits a period or country property better than aluminum. However, the latter is far easier to maintain and keep clean.

Once you have decided on the sort of frame you want, you need to consider size. Decide what you are going to grow and how much space it will take, and then double this figure, as it is inevitable that you will be tempted to grow more. Buy sufficient ventilation and staging for your needs.

The site you choose will play a major part in determining your success. Sunshine is vital, so find a light, open position. You will also need easy access to water and possibly electricity, as you may wish to heat the greenhouse in winter, or use a propagator.

playtime

While parents must be able, for safety reasons, to keep an eye on little children, older children need their own space where they can be free to be adventurous. They love hidden corners, where they can play hide-and-seek, make forts, and pretend they are fearless explorers, so site their play area in a far corner, or give them some feeling of privacy by planting a hedge or building a fence and covering it with climbers.

▶ choosing play equipment

Always buy the best quality you can afford, and always buy from a reputable dealer. Second-hand equipment may be cheaper, but, unless you are buying from a friend you can trust, you cannot be sure of its history or how it has been treated.

Left
Children love being outside in any kind of weather; in the garden, you can let them run around without fear of them crashing into furniture.

Check for sharp edges, protruding nails and screws, and unplaned wood that may splinter. Ensure that equipment you purchase passes all standard safety testing for materials and design. Ask if the product's manufacturer is a member of, and that their products have been approved by, the American Society for Testing Materials (ASTM). And ask if the equipment manufacturer is a member of the International Play Equipment Manufacturer's Association (IPEMA). It is also critical that you follow the manufacturer's assembly directions very carefully for optimal safe usage. All countries run their own safety tests and have symbols to signify that a toy or piece of equipment meets the recommended standard. Also check for age-recommended symbols, because many pieces of equipment are not suitable for children under the age of three.

Regularly examine and maintain play equipment and structures. Make sure free-standing slides, climbing frames, and swings are firmly anchored in the ground and that all nuts and bolts are tight. Buy hard-wearing nylon rope instead of natural fiber, and replace it at the first signs of fraying.

Remember that children are imaginative and unpredictable, and will not necessarily use their play equipment in the way the manufacturer intended. A good general rule is always to expect the unexpected.

To be sure your children have a soft landing if they fall, place play equipment on well-watered grass, safety matting (a material made from recycled tires works well), or, even better, a thick layer of bark or wood chips or sand. It is also advisable to choose a semi-shaded area for any play equipment or structures, so that children are not exposed for long periods to harmful ultraviolet rays.

water and sand

All children love sand and water. This classic seaside combination offers endless opportunities to get wet and dirty, both popular pursuits, especially with children under five. So paddling pools and sandpits will be well used.

If you have the space, a permanent sand play area is worth considering. This can take the form of a pit, or more simply, a box. For a simple sandpit, dig a hole to the desired depth and width, spread a sheet of heavy-duty plastic on the bottom, with holes punched in it for drainage, then fill with children's play sand (not builders' sand). Finish the sandpit with a low wall of pressure-treated wooden stockading, stone, or brick. For a sandbox, spread the plastic on the ground and use four railroad ties as sides. Make sure that the ties are not heavily impregnated with creosote or tar, which will leak out in hot sunshine, making a sticky (and toxic) mess. There are also kits with ready-cut and planed wooden planks that slot together. If you live near the beach, buy an old dingy and use that as your sandpit. It will be very picturesque and look wholly in keeping with the setting.

Two of the most popular designs among the huge range of ready-made sandpits are the plastic boat and the clam shell. These are made in two sections, forming a base and lid, which provide much more flexibility. For example, you can fill the base with sand and the lid with water.

Covers are very important for sandpits. They keep the sand dry, but more importantly keep it clean, preventing animals from fouling it. Use a sheet of fine mesh or oilcloth as a cover for homemade sand play areas, or a fitted wooden lid, if the sandpit forms part of a decked area.

As with sandpits, there are paddling pools to suit all ages of children and sizes of garden—from little ones you blow up, through rigid molded plastic, to large, soft, plastic pools with metal frames. Remember that regardless of the pool you choose, adult supervision is vital.

Water is enjoyable on a hot summer day, so supplement the paddling pool with other water toys, such as bubble machines and water sprinklers. There is a range of random-spray, oscillating water sprinklers that fulfill every criteria for fun. They look bright and cheerful—being disguised as flowers, insects, and animals—and produce a fine, refreshing spray that will cool children down. It is the element of surprise that makes them so enjoyable. Even the most alert child is bound to be caught off-guard and given a soaking. Your plants will love them, too.

Combine a random sprinkler with a water slide and you will find it almost impossible to drag the children indoors at bedtime. To make a simple slide, spread a large sheet of plastic or oilcloth on the ground and make it good and slippery with

Above
Water is always a favorite with young children, and whether you have a water feature they can play in or you simply fill an inexpensive paddling pool, they are bound to love it.

Right
A large pile of sand in a corner of the garden will suffice, but make sure you cover it with a sheet of fine mesh or oilcloth after use to ensure that it stays clean and dry.

Above
Choose play equipment that you can add to as your child grows. Walkways, cable runs, and rope ladders create an adventureous playground heaven.

a sprinkling of water mixed with a few drops of dish soap. If you want a really fast slide, place the plastic on a slight slope.

play structures

Giving children their own space and territory is important for their happiness as well as good family relations. If everyone is on top of each other, irritations soon develop and arguments are inevitable. Private hide-aways and secret forts are an excellent way of providing the sense of adventure and freedom children require within the safety of their garden.

Even before children learn to walk, they are trying to climb, pulling themselves upright by any means available. So what could be better than providing them with the means to indulge this basic instinct. Climbing frames range from a simple structure consisting of two ends connected by a single crossbar, to labyrinths of ladders, walkways, slides, swings, and tunnels. Choose a frame that you can add to, so that it grows with your children, offering new challenges to their developing abilities.

Give some thought to the material the frame is made of, because once it is up, it will be a feature in your garden for years to come. There are many brightly colored metal frames on the market, but there are also more subdued wooden frames available, with dark green attachments rather than vivid red or orange.

If you are lucky enough to have a few sturdy trees, you can attach climbing ropes, rope ladders, commando-style netting, and swings to their branches, which constitute the most natural frame there could be.

Even if you cannot find the space for a climbing frame, it is always possible to fit in a swing—there are even models that can be attached to the wall of a house. Of all play apparatus, swings are unique in that they are equally popular with boys and girls, toddlers and teenagers.

If you do not have a suitable tree, buy or make a frame instead. Aluminum or wooden frames are not expensive and are easy to erect, the only difficulty involving anchoring the legs. These can be secured by pins, but the safest method is to sink them in concrete-filled holes several feet deep.

Make your swing grow with your child by altering the seat. Babies require a high-backed bucket seat with a safety harness and restraining bar at the front. The next stage up is the strap, or belt seat made of soft rubber, which molds itself to the shape of the child's bottom, preventing them from slipping off. For seven-year-olds and up, there is the flat rubber or plank seat.

Both children and grown-ups can be seriously injured if they are hit by a moving swing, so place the swing well away from paths, sandpits, and playhouses, and drill into your children the importance of keeping their distance—you can always mark out an exclusion zone.

trampolines

Young children enjoy sit-on, bouncy, rubber balls and small trampolines, and older children with lots of energy enjoy a full-size trampoline. Be sure that a child or adult stands by while another bounces, and fit cushioned pads over the hard edges of the frame. If you follow a few safety guidelines—one at a time, no shoes or jewelry, no eating and drinking—your children will bounce happily for hours.

▶playhouses

Below
Get children to build their own teepees—all they need are old sheets, bamboo canes, and string. You might need to lend a helping hand to ensure that it doesn't fall down.

Anyone who read *Peter Pan* as a child was probably enchanted by Wendy's little house and wanted one of their own. Wendyhouses, now generally called playhouses, are still popular, as are tents, teepees, treehouses, and forts.

There are many ready-made playhouses available, some with window boxes, little porches, and even upstairs rooms. To add to the charm of these buildings, paint or color-stain them a soft blue-gray or any color that ties in with your overall scheme and decorate simply, perhaps with gingham curtains and a few pots of cheerful pelargoniums.

If you have an old shed that you do not use often, you can transform it into a woodland cabin straight out of the fairy tale *Hansel and Gretel*. Cut logs into thin cross-sections or split larch poles lengthwise and nail them to the outside walls. To complete the picture, plant ivy to grow up the sides and lots of striking leafy plants, such as *Euonymus* or ferns, to disguise the entrance and add to the feeling of mystery.

Alternatively, create a Heidi-inspired look by cutting Tyrolean-style ornamental eaves and shutters out of marine ply and fixing them onto the shed. Add some window boxes, hang checked curtains at the windows, and color-stain or paint.

If your shed is in a leafy corner of the garden, you could try a jungle theme. Attach bamboo screens to the sides of the shed and disguise the roof with a thatch screen, made from woven brushwood. Plant a couple of *Fatsia japonicas*—which have large, glossy, tropical-looking leaves—and place a cut-out, painted plywood tiger so that it is peeping out from behind the vegetation.

No child will be able to resist the charm of a living, albeit temporary, playhouse made from sunflowers and woven willow or hazel switches. Plant the sunflowers, willow, or hazel in a circle, leaving a space for an entrance. As the sunflowers grow, their huge heads will form a natural roof with the willow and hazel. However, you will need to tie the tops together once they have reached a suitable height. To create a living playhouse that will look just as good in winter as summer, use evergreens.

tents and teepees

A garden takes on a completely different atmosphere at night. Children are fascinated by the way darkness transforms the garden, making it almost an alien territory, complete with strange rustlings and calls.

Above

A small hidden area serves the same purpose as a playhouse—as long as children can escape from their parents for a while, they'll be happy!

To really appreciate this, you have to spend a night outside, and the best way to do it is in a tent.

There is something very appealing about sleeping under canvas, with only a sheet of thin fabric between you and the stars. It is something every child should be allowed to experience. To avoid frustration, choose a small, simple-to-erect tent, tough enough to withstand daytime play, so that you will be able to use it as a portable playhouse.

If you have a child approaching the eighth, ninth, or tenth birthday and you don't know what to do, invite a couple of his or her best friends to an outdoor sleep-over, complete with birthday barbecue. No one will get much sleep, but it will be an unforgettable night.

Sometimes it is best to keep things simple, and in the case of teepees, this is definitely so. Children will get just as much enjoyment from a teepee made from bamboo or hazel poles and an old sheet they have painted themselves, as they will from an expensive, name-brand version. However, if your garden is large, why not build a permanent teepee that can double as a climbing frame and eventually as a support for climbing plants.

You will need five treated timber poles for the frame. These must be buried a couple of feet in the ground, preferably in concrete for extra stability, then secured at their tops by threading thin, metal wire through holes drilled for the purpose. Once in place, hang a climbing rope from the top of the teepee and wrap more rope around the sides. Fling an old sheet or blanket over the top when the children want to use it as a hideaway.

treehouses

Build your children a treehouse and you will covet it so much that you will not be able to wait until bedtime, when at last you can climb into it to enjoy the sunset.

The type of treehouse you build will be determined by the type and shape of the tree you use. You may be fortunate enough to have a mature tree with three or four thick branches spreading out from the main trunk. If so, then these will form a stable foundation on which to build.

However, it is more likely that you will need to use wooden posts as supports (sunk a few feet into the ground and buried in concrete), so that the house will be virtually self-supporting, even though it will appear to be sitting up in the tree. Whatever tree you select for a treehouse, be sure that its boughs are healthy and strong and that there is no danger of branches falling from above.

The distance from the treehouse platform to the ground is crucial. Obviously, if your children are very little, you will not want them climbing too high. You must also be sure that the ladder is firmly secured, its treads are not too far apart, and it is not set at too steep an angle. Rope ladders are not suitable for little children.

If your children are very young, you could buy a large wooden doghouse, cut out holes for windows, glaze them with shatter-proof plastic, paint the house a pretty color, and place it in a low-growing tree, such as an apple. It may need extra supports, but its fully enclosed sides make it extremely safe.

Treehouses for older children can be higher and more open and, if the tree allows it, you can build more than one platform or story. Use well-seasoned, treated timber for the supports, base, and cross beams, making sure that it is smooth and free from splinters. Floors, walls, and roofs can be made from sheets of marine ply and the roof covered with shingles or roofing felt. The outside of the treehouse can be softened and camouflaged with woven willow hurdles or clapboarding. You can set up a rope and pulley, so a basket can be lowered to replenish provisions!

▶games

If you use your garden as an outside room, then almost any games can be played there. If your child has a favorite toy, encourage them to take it outside when the weather is fine.

games for the family

There are many traditional games in which all the family can join. Ball games such as baseball, football, and volleyball have delighted generations of children and are equally popular with adults.

Similarly, games requiring a racket, such as badminton and swing ball, will provide hours of entertainment and exercise as well as helping children to concentrate and develop their hand-eye coordination.

Croquet, while more leisurely, is also popular, and is particularly good for the evening, when you are trying to get everyone to wind down.

Even if you live in the country, there is no reason why your children need to miss out on such traditional street games as hopscotch. They can simply mark their squares in chalk on any paved area—the chalk will wash off as soon as it rains. More permanent hopscotch, chess, or checker boards can be made from colored paving slabs (see page 29).

Below
Lawn bowling can be enjoyed by a wide range of ages, and a set is inexpensive.

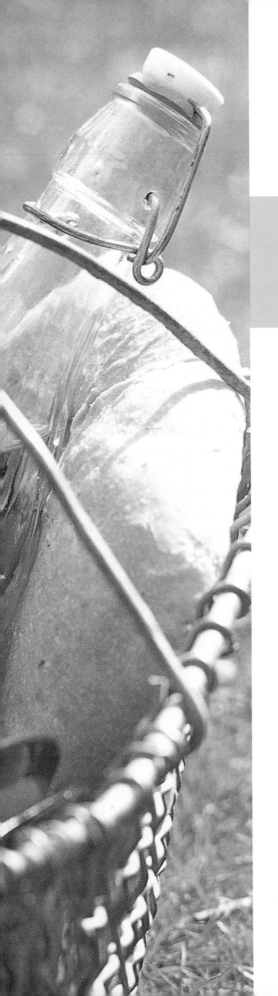

eating
alfresco

Summertime alfresco meals conjure up their own unique ambience. From the promise of a long, heat-hazy day at breakfast time, through to starry evenings among the heady fragrances of night-scented plants, the atmosphere of the garden alters as no interior space can. Whether you enjoy sophisticated, elegant, adult dinner parties or cheerful, noisy, family barbecues, the garden as dining room provides a setting for some truly memorable occasions.

▶dining outdoors

As with all your garden furnishings, your dining furniture should tie in with house and garden style and must suit your needs in terms of sturdiness and ease of storage.

Below
An all-in-one picnic table is inexpensive and stable—ideal for a family garden.

Each material has advantages and disadvantages (see page 40), but your first consideration should be the number of people you will need to seat.

If you cannot find a large enough table within your price range, why not dress up an ordinary table. Office supply shops often have large, sturdy tables with metal legs and wooden tops that are perfectly adaptable for garden use. Choose a color such as dark green, which always looks good outdoors, and then paint the legs and put matching tiles on the tabletop. The result is extremely stylish and will easily weather summer showers, although a plastic cover is advisable for winter.

deciding where to dine

The position of your outdoor dining area will determine how often you use it. If it is too far from the kitchen, eating out will be too much of an effort. However, if the area closest to the kitchen happens to be without shade, exceptionally windy, or down a steep flight of steps, this option is equally unappealing.

Comfort is all important when it comes to eating out. Everyone must feel relaxed, and the dining area must be spacious enough for people to be able to push their chairs back at the end of the meal to talk, cuddle little children on their laps, or just enjoy the garden. As a general rule, an area of 12 square feet (3.6 sq m) should be sufficient.

Shade is also vital. Lunch under a blazing sun takes on the characteristics of an endurance test and is not the relaxed, unhurried affair it should be. Even breakfast can be intolerable if the sun is beating down, hurting your eyes, and melting the butter.

If your garden has no natural shade, buy a canvas umbrella or canopy or, for a really beautiful setting, build an arbor over which you can train climbers.

setting the scene

Once you have picked the ideal site, turn it into a spot where people will want to linger. Containers really come into their own here. Gather together a group of different shapes and sizes and fill them with a good variety of plants. Include some flowering shrubs and small trees—such as *camellia*, peony, and a pretty miniature Japanese maple—to provide a permanent framework, then fill in with tubs or pots of spring and summer-flowering bulbs, a froth of *Nemesia*, daisy-like *Argyranthemum*, or colorful *pelargonium*.

Be sure to include some containers of herbs that can be picked as flavorings or garnishes. And for an after-dinner snack, place a couple of terracotta strawberry pots where diners can reach out and pick the fruit, or plant wild strawberry plants between cracks in the pavers or along the edges of surrounding beds. In warm climates a grape vine (*Vitis vinifera*) adds exotic shade and provides a delicious ready-made dessert.

Think of your outdoor dining area as a theatrical stage set, to be decorated as the mood strikes you. One of the joys of containers is that they can be moved around and replanted easily, so you can constantly change and update your color scheme and create more or less dramatic effects. If you change your table covering and china, you can transform the setting of the meal.

Vary the look of your table by leaving it uncovered for breakfast, covering it with a cheerful gingham tablecloth for lunch, a colorful oilcloth for children's meals, then a dark tablecloth for the grown-ups' dinner. Once in a while you can make a real occasion out of dinner and go all out to create an evening of high drama and glamour. Dress the table with crisp white linen, glinting silver cutlery, and sparkling polished glass; light it with candelabra and lanterns, and you will have a stylish and elegant setting for a dinner party.

▶a feast for all the senses

Once your visual sense is satisfied, do not neglect to feed the other senses. To make your dining area complete, use the power of scent, sound, and touch.

Sound brings an area to life. The sound of trickling water creates a magical ambience, so try to incorporate a wall fountain or bubble pond near to where you plan to eat. The faint, rather mystical music of wind chimes will also add to the atmosphere as long as your garden is not windy, in which case the sound can be tortuous. The rustle of bamboo grasses or broad-leaved plants such as hostas make their own contribution to the garden's atmosphere.

Fill the air with perfume from container-grown plants such as scented leaf *Pelargonium* (*P.* 'Graveolens' or *P.* 'Fragrans'), lilies (such as *Lilium regale* or *longiflorum*), and tobacco plants (*Nicotiana alata*); look for heirloom varieties for best scents. Train climbers such as honeysuckle, jasmine, *Solanum crispum*, or the roses 'New Dawn' or 'Madame Alfred Carriére' up any vertical surface and plant fragrant shrubs such as mock orange (*Philadelphus*), Mexican orange (*Choisya ternata*), or *Viburnum* (*V. carlesii*) nearby.

Finally, add some containers of velvet-petalled pansies to touch, and place a few pots of silky ornamental grasses like *Pennisetum* strategically, where you can run your fingers through them in passing. They will also rustle in a breeze.

Right
The *Ranunculus* in the vase and the *Clematis montana* on the trellis perfume this eating area and coordinate beautifully with the color of the table.

Below
Blackberries grown around this seating area provide a convenient and delicious dessert. Small trees in containers provide privacy.

▶informal eating

Try to drag yourself away from your wonderful dining area from time to time, to experience the joys of eating someplace totally different. This may be underneath a spreading tree or in a quiet corner where the garden looks different.

Above
A table, stools, cushions, and toys on the lawn provide a relaxed and practical setting for children to enjoy eating and playing in the sun.

For truly informal eating, spread out a rug or blanket, or set up a circle of tree stumps as little stools for the children to have an elfin feast. Children's parties work well outdoors. There is no need to worry about spilled drinks or 20 pairs of little hands smearing chocolate all over the walls.

Prepare a picnic basket with individually wrapped sandwiches and fruit to avoid disagreements, and remember that eating outdoors does something miraculous to children's appetites. The daintiest little eater will become a ravenous creature.

Hide little treats around the garden for the children to search for after lunch. This will keep them occupied while the grownups eat their meal. Keep a few of the treats in reserve in case one of the children gets too many and leaves someone empty-handed and tearful.

barbecues

Eating outdoors is even more fun if you cook alfresco as well. There's nothing better than a party of family and friends gathered around tables filled with salads and delicious bread and being tortured by the delicious smells of meat, fish, and vegetables cooking on the grill.

Barbecue grills fall into two different basic categories, built-in and free-standing. Within the second category are several different electric and gas models for those who don't like making a mess, or the traditional charcoal grill—the only choice for the real aficionado.

Free-standing barbecues vary enormously in size, weight, and therefore portability. There are excellent small cast iron models that can be placed on a wall or bricks and that are ideal for a couple of people, or for picnics. For a family, a larger brazier, kettle, or (for really serious barbecuers) rotisserie grill is more suitable.

It is a simple matter to build your own permanent barbecue. To decide on a site, take into account the direction of the prevailing wind, the distance from the kitchen and outdoor dining area, and safety aspects. You will need stone or frost-proof bricks for the three walls and base, and a metal brazier and grill tray. Design the barbecue so that the tray can be easily removed for cleaning, and include enough storage space for fuel, as well as flat surfaces to hold all the utensils, dishes, and bowls you will need while cooking.

Plant lots of herbs around the base of the barbecue and, if it looks a little forlorn in winter, disguise it with containers of plants or an attractive, removable wooden lid.

Eating outdoors seems to enhance flavors, so that the simplest food tastes delicious. Yet it is also fun to experiment with different culinary themes. Thai, Caribbean, Mexican, and Spanish foods all lend themselves to barbecuing. Their spicy, tangy flavors are offset nicely by the bittersweet smokiness that cooking over an open flame produces.

Good planning and timing are essential for success. Meat that is marinated overnight will be more tender and tasty, and certain foods benefit from being started off in the oven. This is especially important for chicken, as nothing is more off-putting and potentially dangerous than being handed a piece of chicken that is virtually black on the outside but still pink and bloody in the middle. Whether you plan to

cook on charcoal or wood, remember to allow sufficient time for the fuel to become hot enough for cooking.

Toward the end of the cooking process, throw a few herbs or slivers of wet wood from fruit trees onto the barbecue to create aromatic smoke.

Certain barbecued foods are guaranteed to be a success with children. Sausages and kebabs are easy to eat, because everything is already in bite-sized pieces, and pork chops marinated overnight in crushed garlic, lemon juice, and olive oil, are likely to be devoured by even the choosiest child.

Fresh fish barbecues well, especially swordfish and tuna, which have good solid, meaty flesh. Sardines and mackerel are also delicious.

Always provide plenty of salads and bread. Other essentials are coleslaw, potato salad, and a Greek salad made from tomatoes, cucumber, and feta cheese in a piquant dressing.

Above

An example of a permanent barbecue. The surrounding, low brick wall makes an ideal flat surface for cooking utensils, dishes, and seating.

garden lighting

Above
A partially concealed spotlight provides discreet lighting and can be angled to shine through the grass to highlight a feature.

Nothing has quite the effect on atmosphere that lighting does. An otherwise plain area can be made wildly romantic with cleverly placed lanterns and candles. Lighting can extend the time for sitting outdoors, can be used to highlight features—such as an interesting tree, fountain, or statue—and extends your enjoyment of the garden during winter evenings when you are looking out from the warmth of the house.

Just as you do with interior lighting, you should think of outdoor lighting fulfilling two basic purposes—one being utilitarian and the other decorative. The former is deployed for safety and security beside driveways, steps, pools, paths, and dining areas, while decorative lighting is used to illuminate interesting features and to provide atmosphere.

Plan the positions of utilitarian lights first, as they are often the simplest to place. Start with your parking and entrances to the house, then consider the dining area, and any steps or paths leading off it down which you may wander in the evening. Paths to a swimming pool, tennis court, wood storage shed, or the garbage can area will need occasional lighting.

If security is a concern, well-placed lights will deter intruders and help the homeowner feel safer. If you are worried about light pollution and saving energy, then lights that switch themselves on when they sense movement are the answer. But be aware that dogs and cats may often trigger these sensors.

Next, turn your attention to decorative lighting. An unusual statue or urn is a perfect candidate to be picked out in a spotlight, and moving water or a gnarled old tree also looks spectacular. The angle of the lighting will give different effects. For example, backlighting produces dramatic silhouettes, uplighting picks out unusual features that you would not notice during the day, while downlighting is closest to daylight.

For the dining area you will need more muted background lighting, to which you can then add, in keeping with the style of meal you are planning.

As with any electrical equipment, garden lighting should be installed by a qualified electrician. For a complex set-up, covered cables may have to be sunk into the ground. Heavy-duty weather-proof cables, which can run along the surface are also

Above
Candles are another option for outdoor lighting. Why not move your indoor candles outside during the evening? Make sure they are not too close to any foliage.

Right
Placing lights near steps makes moving around the garden at night much safer.

Left
A combination of uplighters, spotlights, and candlelight create a magical atmosphere, ideal for evening entertaining.

available: they can be disguised with foliage or chips. These are probably not a good choice for a family garden because they could trip someone, and if accidentally cut, would give an electric shock.

The harsh glare of electric light can destroy the atmosphere of an outside dining area. It is impossible to relax when you are in the glare of a spotlight. People are more at ease when lighting is kept low—although if it is too dim you will find yourself squinting uncomfortably at your plate in an attempt to see just what is on it. Subtle ways of lighting your table include lighting that "grazes" the wall of the house, or that gently uplights nearby foliage.

For alfresco dinners the ideal light is provided by candles. It is soft and flattering, the shadows are not as defined as those cast by electric light, and the candlelight has warmth and life to it.

Lanterns solve the problem of a breezy patio with sputtering candles. There are many different types—old-fashioned storm lanterns, hurricane lights, Indian-style brass lamps with star-shaped holes punched in them, or antique-style, glass, jam jars containing nightlights. These can sit on the table or hang from metal stakes stuck in the ground. The variety of candle holders and protective containers is endless.

If you want to make the evening electricity-free from start to finish, guide your guests to the table along a pathway of large garden candles or paraffin-fuelled, oriental, bamboo torches stuck in the ground.

Many candles and lanterns perform a dual function—providing light while discouraging insects. For example, the scent of citronella is attractive to humans but hated by insects, and insects find lanterns with orange-colored glass less alluring than those with clear glass. There are also lanterns that emit ultraviolet light. This attracts the insects and then electrocutes them as they land on the element. A few of these placed in a circle a discreet distance from the table should ensure a bite-free evening for everyone.

outdoor heating

Outdoor heaters and portable fireplaces have long been popular in Scandinavian countries. There are large, overhead, electric bar heaters and free-standing, portable, electric, convector models. But it is easy to build your own outdoor hearth or to use a barbecue as a raised fireplace. If you pile on lots of fuel and light it well before you plan to eat, it should be red-hot by the time you sit down.

animals

Most children are fascinated by animals, and if you can encourage this fascination you will not only give your children an interest that will stay with them for life, but one that is educational and will teach them about responsibility and caring for others.

▶ family pets

The size of your house and garden will help determine what animal is suitable for your family. An urban house with a small garden is hardly the best place for a goat or an enormous dog.

inside or out?

Certain pets are happy living outdoors for most of the year, depending on the severity of the climate. Rabbits and guinea pigs can cope with fairly harsh weather as long as they have a water-tight, draft-proof hutch with plenty of bedding material to keep them warm. The hutch should have a large run attached as they like lots of exercise. Cats and dogs need access to a garden, but

other pets such as mice, gerbils, and hamsters also enjoy an occasional trip outside. However, they must be kept inside their cages or they will soon vanish.

escape-proof garden

It is virtually impossible to make your garden totally escape-proof, unless you surround it with a high wire fence and bury the base deep underground. Cats, rabbits, pigs, and goats are seasoned escapees. And foxes, woodchucks, deer, raccoons, and wild rabbits will almost always be able to find a way in. So never let domestic rabbits have the run of the garden and keep goats on a leash, but allow cats freedom to roam. To contain small livestock, a thick hedge supplemented with an electric fence should be sufficient. Be sure the hutch is very secure—not only to prevent your pets from escaping, but also to prevent predators such as cats or foxes from getting at them.

Below
You can disguise a kennel or hutch by training climbers over the top to blend it into the surroundings.

▶butterflies, bees, and other insects

Below
Don't forget to plant *Buddleia davidii.* It is so popular with butterflies that it is commonly called the butterfly bush.

Every garden has a wide selection of insects, some more welcome than others. High on the list of the "goodies" of the insect kingdom are bees, whether honey or bumble, and hoverflies, dragonflies, lacewings, and ladybirds. So if your insects tend to be of the pest variety, it is worth making an effort to attract some of the friendlier kinds.

No matter how many insects you have in the garden, you can never have enough butterflies. It is not only their beautiful colors and prettily shaped wings that are appealing, but their delicate fluttering flight as well. Luckily, the flowers that butterflies prefer are just as pretty and so are worthy of a place in any garden. The only possible exceptions are nettles, which are important for many varieties of butterfly because they lay their eggs on the leaves. So if you want to have beautiful butterflies gracing your garden, it is probably worth gritting your teeth and allowing a clump of nettles to grow in an out-of-the-way corner.

Another thing to remember is that butterflies, being light-bodied insects, cannot stand the wind and prefer sunny, sheltered spots. So if your garden is windswept, it will be necessary to grow a hedge as a windbreak. When you have created your suntrap, either dig out a bed, or group together a selection of containers planted with colorful, fragrant plants. You will not only have a butterfly garden but a delightful place to eat out or simply sit and enjoy the comings and goings of the insects.

The needs of bees and other helpful insects are very similar to those of butterflies. They too are drawn to colorful, fragrant, nectar-rich flowers. Nectar is absolutely vital to the well-being of many flying insects, because it provides them with energy-giving carbohydrates.

Herbs are also guaranteed to attract butterflies, bees, and hoverflies, none of which can resist their strong aroma. Plant lavender, sage, thyme, rosemary, and mint for fragrance, beauty, and a host of attractive visitors. Other good choices are traditional cottage garden-style flowers such as catmint (*Nepeta*), sunflower (*Helianthus*), Aster, anemone, globe thistle (*Echinops ritro*), *Sedum*, and purple coneflower (*Echinarea purpurea*). Many insects, including butterflies and bees, find blue flowers particularly alluring, so include plenty of these when planning a butterfly/ insect corner. Like birds, butterflies and other insects love to feed on rotting fruit, as it ferments, so leave some windfalls.

plants

It is remarkable how different plants can alter the look of a garden and the house attached to it. Apart from the joys of color, perfume, sound, and texture, this is one of the most exciting things about a garden—the opportunity they give their owners to display their personality.

A look around any modern housing development will confirm this. Although the houses and their plots may be identical on paper, the hard work and imagination expended on their gardens makes each as individual as its owner. One garden may show a Japanese influence, with raked gravel, bamboos, and wind chimes exuding an atmosphere of Zen-like calm, simplicity, and control, while next door a profusion of country cottage-style planting creates a feeling of cheerful abundance.

▶gardening for children

Children usually start off full of enthusiasm for gardening, but if they fail to get results, or if the results take too long to appear, they will quickly become disillusioned and lose interest. To ensure that this does not happen, it is important to give them a good set of tools, a sheltered sunny site, and good soil in which things will grow well.

Don't try to palm them off with a dry, shady corner you can't think of anything else to do with. If you encourage a love of gardening when your children are young, it will stay with them for a lifetime.

Once you have chosen a mutually agreeable site, help your child to prepare it. Make sure the soil is well conditioned, adding compost and manure as necessary, and do the heavy digging yourself.

When the children are choosing what to plant, gently direct them away from anything that requires too much attention and suggest they select mainly fast-growing, hardy plants, with a few playful ones, such as snapdragons (*Antirrhinum*), thrown in for fun. To get the garden started, buy some bedding plants, such as pretty *Lobelia*, *Begonia*, *Petunia* or vivid

to experiment with strange colors or combinations of plants.

Some dramatic plants should be included in the garden. Children will delight in the size of pumpkins and the fantastic colors and strange shapes of gourds. Giant watermelons are always fun, while the ultimate novelty in any garden is sunflowers, which can reach great heights. Very little children may find the giant variety just too tall and may have more fun with smaller varieties closer to their own height. These will be more manageable, yet still tall enough to create an *Alice in Wonderland* feel.

When choosing packets of seeds, steer children toward plants with large seeds that are easy to handle and can be relied on to give a good display, such as nasturtium (*Tropaeoleum*), sunflower (*Helianthus*), and Morning Glory (*Ipomoea*).

Other flowers that grow well from seed are the ever-popular sweet pea (*Lathyrus*)—an excellent choice, since it loves to be cut—marigolds (*Tagetes*), love-in-a-mist (*Nigella*), (*Papaver*), cornflowers (*Centaurea cyanus*), and foxgloves (*Digitalis*). In fact, foxgloves are a must for any child brought up on the stories of Beatrix Potter. Many

Above
Foxgloves grow exceptionally well from seed and have a particular relevance to any child brought up on the stories of Beatrix Potter.

Above, far left
Allocate a large container as a garden for your child to look after.

Left
Help your child with the initial planting; do it in stages so that it doesn't seem too much like hard work.

Right
Young children will have hours of fun with their own miniature wheelbarrow and tools, even if they don't actually do any gardening!

Zinnia, pansy, and Impatiens for shady sites. These can be put in pots, used to edge the beds, or planted so that they spell out the child's name.

Give children full rein when it comes to choosing colors. They may choose vivid, clashing combinations, but it is important that they feel their garden is really theirs if they are going to develop enthusiasm for gardening. Grown-ups should allow them

roses

Many roses are unsuitable for a family garden because of their thorns. Here is a selection that are kinder to small fingers.

Thornless

Rosa 'Zéphirine Drouhin.' Deep, magenta pink, perfumed flowers. Long summer to autumn flowering period. Is best on a north-facing wall.

R. 'Kathleen Harrop.' A fragrant climber with shell-pink flowers.

R. 'Goldfinch.' A vigorous rambler that produces small, creamy-yellow blooms in summer.

A few thorns

R. 'America.' Vigorous climbing rose with large, coral pink flowers. Spicy fragrance and long flowering period.

R. 'Souvenir du Dr Jamain.' A climber with deep purple blooms and a very strong fragrance. Likes shade.

R. 'Ghislaine de Feligonde.' A rambler that flowers all year, with apricot-colored blooms. Any thorns will be on the reverse of the leaves.

nurseries and garden centers sell seed mixes especially formulated for children, and these generally offer excellent value for the money.

A few bulbs are always a good addition to any garden, because they are extremely undemanding and children are fascinated by the way these lifeless-looking, papery, underground lumps suddenly burst into bloom. Any selection should include a few early spring bulbs to build up anticipation for the start of the gardening year, as well as some that flower in autumn as a final flourish to round off the season.

Excellent spring bulbs are *Scilla*, *Iris reticulata*, grape hyacinth (*Muscari*), tulips, daffodils, and that harbinger of spring, the crocus. All these bulbs produce small flowers that are extremely pretty and appeal to children's love of the miniature. Reliable autumn performers include many varieties of *Crocus*, *Colchicum*, *Sternbergia*, *Nerine*, and *Cyclamen*. Though all of these are small and delicate-looking, they are actually extremely tough.

Once the children's garden is planted, they should not feel you are constantly inspecting their efforts and interfering,

Left
Lavender is a versatile and easy plant to grow. It will grow well in a container or in a flower bed, and many varieties are hardy so they can be left out during the winter. You can pick the stems and flowers to make lavender filled bags.

Right
Whatever the weather, children will enjoy being outside, even helping with everyday jobs such as digging and removing weeds.

Below
A willow pyramid placed over a box plant (*Buxus*) makes an interesting focal point in a flower bed.

how to make a pyramid

An interesting project for an older child is a topiary pyramid. However, this should only be undertaken with adult supervision as it involves using garden shears. Pyramids look extremely impressive flanking a flight of steps or a bench, and positioned in a border as a focal point.

You can use privet (*Ligustrum*), box (*Buxus*), yew (*Taxus*), rosemary (*Rosmarinus*), hornbeam (*Carpinus betulus*), or holly (*Ilex*).

1 Take eight small garden canes or willow switches and tie the frame together with twine.

2 Spread the canes or switches to form a pyramid.

3 Plant your chosen shrub in a pot or in a bed, then place the frame over it, pushing the canes down into the soil.

4 As the plant grows larger, its shoots will start to push through the pyramid. Trim these back.

5 Once the plant has grown large enough to fill the frame, simply pull the pyramid off.

although a little discreet help, such as occasional watering, will probably be appreciated.

Children have extremely good sensory perception and particularly appreciate plants that have satisfying scents, colors, textures, or even sounds.

The rustling of bamboo stems and leaves and the whispering of ornamental grasses have a particularly strong appeal. Children's hearing is much more sensitive than adults; many young children can even hear the high-pitched navigational squeaks of bats that are totally beyond an adult's hearing range.

It is also important to appeal to the sense of touch. Children love plants that have interesting textures or strokable flowers, leaves, or bark. Silver, velvety-leaved lamb's ear (*Stachys byzantina*), fluffy fennel (*Foemiculum vulgare*), and wormwood (*Artemesia*), or the silky petals of tulips are all popular. Many trees appeal to a child's

sense of touch. The pussy willow (*Salix caprea*) has fluffy catkins, the Himalyan silver birch (*Betula utilis jacquemontii*) and Chinese cherry (*Prunus serrula*) both have satiny bark, while the bark of the maple variety *Acer griseum* is as thin as fine paper and can be peeled off without harming the tree.

Anyone who has witnessed the uncanny ability of children to track down a piece of chocolate wherever it is hidden in the house, will testify to their powerful sense of smell. The garden offers endless opportunities for enticing smells and fragrances that are attractive to young noses.

Children will revel in the heady smell of the white tobacco plant (*Nicotiana alata*) that releases its fragrance at dusk. And the smells of sweet rocket (*Hesperis matronalis*) and stock (*Matthiola*) are guaranteed to delight.

For more unexpected smells, encourage children to plant chocolate cosmos (*Cosmos atrosangiuneus*). In addition to having unusual dark flowers and velvety petals, it releases a strong smell of chocolate. However, it is a tender perennial that needs a sheltered, frost-free, and sunny location. The curry plant (*Helichrysum italicum*) is also surprising with its distinct, unexpected aroma of curry.

Encourage children to collect lavender flowerheads, rose petals, and other aromatic flowers and herbs. These can be dried and made into lavender bags, potpourri, or ribbon-tied bunches of culinary herbs, which they can give away as presents. A really exciting present to grow that will impress even the most sophisticated adult is false topiary. These pieces look astonishingly difficult to produce, but are actually simple. To produce a spiral, bird, or other similar small design, buy a readymade wire frame for it to climb. As the ivy grows, it will cover the frame, eventually hiding it altogether.

Above
Chocolate cosmos: The name alone will interest children, and it also smells of chocolate.

Above
Snowdrops will be one of the first flowers to appear each year.

Right
Lamb's tongue has wonderful, silky leaves that children will love to touch.

Far right
Ornamental grasses add interest because they rustle in the breeze.

▶herbs, fruit, and vegetables

The wonderful thing about herbs, fruit, and vegetables is that there are varieties to suit every situation, from a small pot on a windowsill to a vast acreage. Even if your family has just a tiny balcony, your children can enjoy the pleasure of growing and harvesting their own crop.

Aside from health issues, and the fact that nothing compares with the taste of really fresh produce, there is something primal about the thrill of plucking a piece of fruit off a tree or digging up some home-grown vegetables. It is a thousand times more exciting than a trip to the supermarket and a pleasure that is undiminished by repetition.

Children derive great pleasure from harvesting fruit and vegetables. It is very satisfying to fill a basket with your own produce, and the way root vegetables, such as potatoes and carrots, appear as the soil is turned is magical to a child.

designing a kitchen garden

Some people like to grow their fruits and vegetables in neat, regimented rows, while others prefer to spice the design up a bit by digging out unusual-shaped beds, such as those found in a kitchen garden or potager.

The word potager originated in France, where herbs, vegetables, and flowers have long been grown together. The beauty of a potager does not stem solely from what is grown, but from the way it is laid out.

The design may be a simple grid pattern of four square beds with gravel, brick, or grass paths between, or a more complicated geometric look—perhaps a circle, with segments radiating out from a centerpiece, such as a sundial or obelisk.

The advantage of a potager is that it looks ornamental rather than simply utilitarian. An attractive design is worth positioning it where it can be seen from the house. In a small space where there is no

Right
Tomatoes are one of
the easiest plants to
grow. Their bright red
and orange fruit add
color to a garden and
they taste fantastic.

room for a separate vegetable garden, an upper window may be the vantage point from which the patterns of the beds can best be appreciated.

growing edible plants

Everyone has their favorite fruits and vegetables, but as a general rule it is a good idea to grow things that are either relatively rare or expensive to buy. Vegetables in season are often cheaper to buy in the supermarket than to grow at home, so choose a few crops that are quick to mature and some with a longer growing season, such as squashes, spinach, and the more exotic varieties of lettuce. It's possible to extend your harvest by staggering the times of sowing, ensuring that the crops ripen in succession and you don't end up with a glut of one vegetable.

If the garden is very small, grow herbs, fruit, and vegetables in flower borders. Small plants, such as fluffy-headed carrots and leafy lettuces, should be placed at the front of the beds, with delicate fronds of fennel and asparagus and the large leaves of rhubarb behind, and at the back of the border the tallest vegetables such as globe artichokes (*Cynara scolymus*). Plant peas and beans to scramble up a fence or make a feature of cane teepees for these and other climbing plants.

Many herbs, fruit, and vegetables are so decorative that it is worth growing them on their own in containers so that their shapes and colors can be fully appreciated. Plant a frilly-leaved lettuce in a pot, or place a colorful miniature pepper plant on a table as a centerpiece. Squashes are easy to grow and have glorious, trumpet-shaped, yellow blooms.

Be sure to include fruit and vegetables that children can snack on, such as peas—which always taste sweetest when picked straight from the pod—and little cherry tomatoes. Alpine strawberries are also an excellent choice. Plant these as edging around your vegetable beds, then send the children out after lunch to pick their dessert. They will be happy for a long time, searching for the delicious, succulent little fruit.

While tiny alpine strawberries may escape the full attention of birds, it is unlikely that other soft fruit will be so lucky. So if you are planning to grow redcurrants, raspberries, or blackcurrants and

Above
Herbs, fruit, and vegetables all grow well in containers.

Below
Encourage your child to plant seeds so that they can see a plant grow from scratch. Use a transparent container so they can see the roots growing as well.

do not want to share the fruit of your labors with every bird for miles around. then it is worth growing them in a fruit cage. These are simple constructions made of netting and posts that can be bought ready-made. then taken down and stored at the end of the growing season. Check carefully from time to time to make sure that there are no tears or gaps in the netting. because small birds can easily become trapped inside.

There are many new varieties of fruit that allow gardeners with even very small gardens to enjoy picking their own. Look

for dwarf trees and the very slim ballerina breeds. You can maximize space by training trees to grow into fan shapes against the house as espaliers. or as "fences" dividing the garden.

Like fruit and vegetables. herbs demand a sunny. sheltered spot with well-drained soil. Yet they are happy to grow among the flowers and plants in borders. with fruit and vegetables. alone in a formal herb garden. or in pots on the patio.

Herbs are important for more than their flavors. Many have extremely pretty flowers and foliage. are wonderfully aromatic. and attract all kinds of insects. especially bees and butterflies (see page 85).

The most basic selection of herbs for the family garden includes rosemary. lavender. mint. parsley. sage. and thyme. In addition. try to find space for coriander. oregano. and basil. which all look extremely pretty and have a delicious fragrance and taste. Mint is very invasive. so if you want to include it in a border or herb garden. plant it in a container sunk into the soil. to prevent the roots from spreading.

A formal herb garden adds a special touch to any space and can be quite small. Like medieval European monks. early American settlers grew herbs for medicinal as well as culinary purposes and favored a simple square or rectangular shape intersected by a path in the shape of a cross with an island bed in the center. A beehive may originally have been placed on this island. but nowadays a sundial or obelisk is more practical. Such a design could easily be copied in a space of no more than a few square yards or meters.

In the past. herbs have also been used as dyes. and children can have a great time experimenting with these. Most people are familiar with the wonderful blue that comes from indigo. but less well known is the fact that sorrel yields an unusual greeny-yellow dye and that a good yellow comes from marigolds.

dangerous plants

Below
Rue is an irritant, so if you find this growing in your garden, it is advisable to remove it.

Babies and young children love to put things in their mouths. Young babies, not being very mobile, will happily make do with whatever is immediately at hand. Soil, pebbles, the odd insect, all will be carefully tasted, chewed, and then, hopefully, spat out.

As they get older and more mobile, children widen the range of the inedibles they attempt to eat. Anything colorful, especially berries, is tempting, but because many of these are poisonous the potential for disaster is considerable.

Set aside a couple of hours, arm yourself with a list of dangerous plants, and take a stroll around your garden. You'll be amazed at the results of your survey. Many of the most commonly grown plants, such as foxgloves and lupins, are poisonous, but they don't pose much of a risk because few children would ever be tempted to eat them. It is the plants and trees with berries that pose the bigger problem. Most children cannot distinguish between blackcurrants and deadly nightshade or between laburnum seed pods and pea pods, and are likely to think that anything that looks like food must be food.

The first thing to do is to train your children from the earliest age never to put things in their mouths or to eat anything unless you have specifically stated that it is safe. Next, remove as many poisonous plants from your garden as possible, fence off any others that you want to keep, and make a real effort to remove berries that fall on the ground.

If you find that your child has been eating something poisonous, check to be sure that there is not any plant matter left in the mouth, then seek medical advice. Remember to take a sample of the plant with you if you go to the doctor's office or hospital. Do not try to make the child vomit.

When conducting your survey of the garden, also look for plants and weeds that cause skin rashes and allergies. When children tear around a garden, they are likely to brush against plants that may have irritating leaves, stems, or sap.

It is well known that weeds such as poison ivy cause rashes, but there are many cultivated plants capable of causing

similar if not worse skin reactions. Most dangerous of all are the plants with photo-sensitive sap that, when exposed to sunlight, triggers a chemical reaction that makes the sap irritating.

Giant hogweed (*Heracleum mantegazzianum*) is a common example of such a plant. It is very architectural, with its spreading white umbrella flowers on top of tall woody stems. But it should be excluded from any garden where children play, because there have been many cases of children using these hollow woody stems as pea shooters and then developing blisters around their mouths as soon as they go into the sunlight. The blisters can last for weeks,

Above
Giant hogweed.

Right
Monkshood
(*Aconitum* species).

Above
Castor-oil plant
(*Ricinus communis*).

Above
Blackthorn shrubs bear
sloe berries, which
make good drinks, but
the plant isn't suitable
for young children
because of its thorns.

Above
Firethorn (*Pyracantha*)
has attractive berries
and is very hardy, but it
has thorns so it's best
to keep it out of reach
of young children.

while the underlying damage to the skin
may not be repaired for months.

Other common garden plants that can
cause serious skin problems include the
spurges (*Euphorbia*), rue (*Ruta* and
species), monkshood (*Aconitum* and
species), poison hemlock (*Conium mac-
ulatum*), *Colchicum* and species, and the
castor-oil plant (*Ricinus communis*).
Place such plants at the back of the borders, where children are less likely to
come in contact with them, and warn
them of the danger.

Plants with spikes and thorns are a danger to children. *Berberis*, *Pyracantha*, and
hawthorns (*Crataegus*) all have long, sharp
thorns, and *Mahonia* and holly leaves are
very spiky, especially once they have fallen
to the ground to dry out. The tips of yucca
leaves have strong, sharp spikes, and most
varieties of roses and blackberries have
thorns. It would be a shame to ban these
attractive plants from the garden, so they
should be doctored—for example, by snip-
ping the tips off the yucca and placing them
where they are out of the reach of children.

▶resilient
plants

While some plants may pose a danger to children, it is more more often children who pose a danger (and a deadly one at that) to plants. A vigorous game of soccer in the wrong place can be very destructive.

Below
Geraniums and Lady's Mantle are great plants that grow quickly and can survive occasional mishaps.

To avoid worrying about the damage that is being done to your plants every time the children go out to play, design your garden so that the planting around the children's main play area comprises only the most hardy, vigorous, and forgiving plants and shrubs. Anything at all delicate should be moved to another part of the garden, where it can grow in peace.

If you have grass, be sure that it is a hardy variety and do not cut it lower than ½ to 1 inch (1.2 to 2.5 cm). Grow low and medium height perenniels that will happily regenerate themselves. Perenniel geraniums are particularly recommended. They spread freely and are so hardy that they can easily cope with an occasional trampling. Similarly, ivies (*Hedera*) are extremely tough and recover quickly after being crushed or having strands ripped off for crowns or garlands.

Some flowers, such as foxgloves (*Digitalis*) and poppies (*Papaver*), actually benefit from being brushed against and having the ground around them disturbed, because this helps to spread their seeds over a wider area. Lady's mantle (*Alchemilla mollis*) is also a prodigious self-seeder that will quickly recover from any damage it sustains.

Of the shrubs, Butterfly bush (*Buddleia*) is virtually indestructible and will soon recover even if whole branches have been ripped off. *Viburnum* and *Euonymus* also cope well with rough treatment, and mallows (*Lavatera*) will continue to produce their wonderful stems of hollyhock-like flowers almost as fast as children can pick them.

Privet (*Ligustrum*) is another useful shrub. Besides being extremely tough, it makes a dense hedge, ideal for separating areas of the garden, and can be cut into all sorts of shapes if you want to experiment with topiary. Finally, its cuttings can be used to feed any stick insects the children may be keeping as pets.

▶low maintenance gardening

For many families, especially those with very young children, life is a constant race against time. In addition to work, school, and socializing, there may be ballet, swimming, soccer, and other extra-curricular activities to fit into the day.

Right
A busy family life
leaves little time for
gardening, but if you
make it a family
activity, it will seem
like less of a chore.

The fact is that many of us simply do not have much time to spend lavishing attention on a garden.

There are a number of things you can do to minimize the need for constant maintenance, yet still have an attractive garden that flourishes from year to year.

Aim for an uncomplicated natural layout, because anything too formal demands a great deal of attention to keep it looking trim. Avoid annual bedding plants that need to be dug up at the end of each season, and instead choose plants that will take care of themselves.

Bulbs and perennials appear year after year and, despite advice in many gardening books that they should be dug up and divided after blooming, will happily repeat their display with virtually no attention at all. Better still, numerous plants, such as anemone, dead nettle (*Lamium*), periwinkle (*Vincas*), and geranium, provide good-looking ground covers that spread vigorously without any human assistance and smother weeds at the same time.

Choose shrubs, especially evergreens, that naturally grow into an attractive shape and eliminate the need to spend hours clipping and training. Plant climbers that are self-clinging rather than twining, so that you do not need a trellis or wires to tie them on.

Lawns are relatively high maintenance areas because they require regular mowing, but the open space is very useful in a family garden. Instead of converting your lawn to paving or gravel, create a brick or paved area flush with the soil surface, so that the mower will be able to cut right to the edge and you will be able to avoid the back-breaking chore of edging with shears.

Containers look pretty, but keep them to a minimum, because they are labor-intensive, requiring constant watering in dry weather and re-potting at the start of each season.

Soft fruit and vegetables also require a lot of attention, so don't be too ambitious until the children are old enough not to pose a risk to containers and plants. Consider installing an automatic watering system (see page 52). These are invaluable for anyone who does not have much time to spend on the garden.

recycling

How green is your garden? A garden gives ample scope to indulge green tendencies in more ways than one. Gardeners who cannot be bothered to recycle organic waste, such as dead plant matter and household items, ignore a valuable resource. They are depriving their garden of nourishing food and creating more work for themselves in the process.

▶compost

Compost is a dark, rich, sweet-smelling, crumbly substance that improves soil condition by adding water-retaining humus and nitrogen—vital for the well-being of plants.

Above
Set aside a corner of the garden for a compost pile. All kinds of natural waste, from coffee grounds to chopped grass, can be composted and recycled into the garden.

Compost can be bought, but it's so easy to make that there is little excuse for not doing so. There is a two-fold advantage to making your own compost. First, you are creating something that will improve the garden immeasurably at no cost and, second, you are making good use of your waste and not taking up valuable space in a landfill site. Dig the compost into your soil, or spread it over the surface when the soil is damp, to act as a mulch.

Virtually any organic material can be composted. From the house, collect coffee grounds and filters, vegetable peelings, eggshells, shredded newspaper, even old cotton or woolen rags. And from the garden, save waste such as dead flowers and leaves, worm-eaten vegetables and old bedding plants, grass clippings, soft prunings, hedge trimmings, and weeds (before they have set seed). The children can help by collecting their pets' droppings when they clean out their cages. These will heat things up, speeding the process of decomposition.

Do not compost meat, cooked food, dairy products, or anything greasy, as these items will attract vermin. Discard and burn the diseased parts of plants, seed-bearing annual weeds, or the roots of perennial weeds, such as ground elder (*Aegopodium podagraria*), couch grass, or quack grass (*Agropyron repens*). These are so tough that they can survive the composting process and you will end up spreading your problems. Anything too woody will not decompose, so either use a shredder or burn such material.

If space allows, create two piles or use two bins. This will ensure a constant supply of compost, since material can be rotting down in one bin while you are still filling the other.

traditional compost heaps

There are many ways of making compost. Compost piles work well in large gardens that produce lots of waste. But completely unenclosed piles are messy and inefficient, so it is better to buy or make an enclosure. Do-it-yourself enclosures can be made from wooden platforms and wire, or you can buy kits to make brick and wood bins or slatted timber enclosures.

With semi-enclosed piles like these, the material at the edges, where it is cooler, will not compost at the same rate as that in the middle, so the pile will need to be turned regularly. Cover it with a sheet of polyethylene or old carpet to keep off heavy rain, but do not allow the pile to dry out in summer. To ensure that there is enough material to heat up sufficiently, the pile or bin must be a minimum of 3 feet (90 cm) square by 4 feet (1.2 m).

Above
You can disguise a compost bin by making or buying a cover. One with slats will allow air to circulate.

Above
Use natural kitchen waste in your compost, such as peelings, eggshells, and shredded newspaper, but don't add greasy food or meat.

ready-made compost bins

If you do not want to make a compost enclosure yourself, there are lots of ready-made plastic and metal bins on the market. These are usually fully enclosed, which means that the composted material will heat up evenly and rot down quickly, eliminating the need to turn the compost. The bins are also designed for ease of access to the composted material at the bottom.

worm bins

These differ from ready-made compost bins in that they rely on a colony of worms (red or red wriggler worms) to produce the compost. The worms are put in specially designed worm bins on a layer of material that has already rotted down. They are then given fresh supplies of finely chopped household scraps every few days.

These bins have a tray to collect liquid, which can be drained off, diluted with water, and used for plant food. The resulting compost is very rich. There are disadvantages to this system, however. Worm bins are not easy to get started, the worms need regular supplies, and the worms must be sieved out when the bin is full and it is time to start a new one—not a pleasant task.

leaf mold

The fallen leaves of deciduous trees, especially oak, beech, and elm, make wonderful compost. Put large piles of leaves in a corner or leaf bin. This is basically a wire cage, and is very simple to make from a roll of chicken wire and four wooden posts. Put smaller piles of leaves into black plastic bags, close them, and punch holes in the sides. The leaves will take about a year to rot down, but you can speed up the process by shredding them and using a leaf compost activator.

making compost

• Start with a thick base of rough, bulky material, such as straw or shredded prunings, then sprinkle with either sulphate of ammonia (a teaspoon per square yard or meter), a commercial compost activator, or fresh animal manure to speed up decomposition.
• Continue building up the heap in 6-inch (15-cm) layers, adding a little lime to alternate layers if you want. Avoid adding too much of any one thing at a time. For example, too many grass clippings can result in a smelly, black slime rather than the sweet, crumbling consistency formed by successful composting.

green compost

Green compost uses living plants, which are grown solely to be dug back into the soil to condition it. Green compost works well for light sandy or heavy clay soils and has the added benefit of demanding less effort than collecting, turning, and spreading home-made compost. Sow the crop to be composted in late summer, cut it just as it flowers in early spring, and allow it to lie for a few days. Then turn it under and leave for a couple of months before planting something else.

Plants that adds lots of nitrogen to the soil are alsike clover (*Trifolium hybridum*), alfalfa, and lupins (*Lupinus*), but borage (*Borago officinalis*), mustard (*Brassica rapa* or *B. nigra*), and comfrey (*Symphytum officinale*) also make excellent green manures.

One obvious disadvantage of green composting is that the soil cannot be used for any other plants while the cover crop is growing. However, if you choose a pretty green compost, this need not be a problem.

▶ inorganic recycling

Below
Construct a drip-
watering system
using old plastic bottles
and rubber tubes.

Most families generate a lot of waste, a large quantity of which is inorganic. With a bit of imagination, however, much of it can be recycled.

Old pots can be pushed sidewise into a hedge for small birds to nest in, a chipped mug can be hung up as a birdfeeder, old carpet can be used on top of the compost heap to help the ingredients heat up, and plastic film cannisters are perfect for storing seeds, since they're dark and airtight.

Polystyrene packing peanuts make an excellent alternative to rocks as drainage material in containers. In fact, if you are planting containers for a balcony or roof garden, polystyrene is ideal, because it is so

light that it greatly reduces the weight of the containers.

Virtually anything that can hold water can be used as a plant container, from ancient rubber boots to old tin tubs, plastic buckets, and pottery. Be careful not to over-clutter your garden, however. It's best to tuck these items away in foliage, so that you come upon them by surprise.

artificial mulches

Pieces of old carpet, thick layers of news-paper, plastic fertilizer bags, and sheets of plastic or cardboard can all be used to clear an area of obstinate weeds. Just cover the ground and leave it alone for a year. Depriving the soil of light means that noth-ing will be able to grow and all the troublesome weeds will die. Disguise your mulching material with gravel or bark if it looks too ugly.

water features

Old pots and pans, baking trays, over-turned garbage can lids, and small buckets are all excellent candidates for transforma-tion into miniature water features. They

making a scarecrow

A scarecrow will not only keep the birds from doing damage to the garden but will provide an amusing focal point and a fun project for the children. If it is moved every once in a while and given a change of clothes, the birds will not have a chance to get used to it.

1 Use an old broom handle or mop as the upright, and a thick woody branch as the horizontal. Or, make a frame by tying together some hazel switches or other flexible stems in a tall cross shape.

2 The head can be a pumpkin or cabbage topped with an old hat.

3 Clothe the scarecrow in an old shirt or jacket and pair of pants, and finish it off with a pair of boots and a scarf.

For an additional bird-scaring touch, give your scarecrow some tin-foil streamers or a mirror to hold, to reflect the sun's rays.

Above

Almost anything can be used as a container for plants. Add a few holes for drainage and plant as normal.

can either be left unplanted as informal bird baths, or they can be planted to make perfect small-scale habitats that will attract wild visitors. Don't forget to keep the water very shallow if you have small children.

watering systems

A cheap way to install an automatic watering system is to make your own discreet watering device out of an old plastic soda bottle.

1) Cut a hole in the base of the bottle just large enough to pour water through.

2) Loosen the cap of the bottle, then place it upside down in the pot so the base of the bottle just pokes above the surface of the compost.

3) Fill the bottle with water through the hole in the base and it will slowly seep out of the loosened cap, providing your thirsty plants with just the right amount of water that they need.

Alternatively, cut an old plastic soda bottle in half. Make three or four small holes in the base, then stick it in a grow-bag of, for example, tomatoes (very thirsty plants). Fill the half-bottle with water and it will slowly trickle through the holes, ensuring that the tomatoes never dry out.

It is also possible to buy specially made spikes that fit on the top of a large plastic soda bottle. Once the bottle is inverted, you can stick the spikes into the ground and they will release water or liquid nutrients slowly through their little holes. Because the spikes penetrate deep into the ground, the water or feed will be able to reach plant roots.

a lacewing home

The larvae of lacewings are a gardener's true friends, because they prey on aphids. To boost your garden's lacewing population, create a comfortable place for them to breed. Take a plastic soda bottle and cut off the base. Next, roll up a sheet of corrugated paper and insert it into the bottomless bottle, securing it with large paper clips or wire. Hang the bottle up in a tree for the winter, and the lacewings should lay eggs in it.

homemade cloches

Glass cloches are now classified as antiques and have high pricetags. There are cheaper plastic alternatives available, but if you need to cover a whole row of plants, these can also be rather expensive. An alternative is to use glass jars for emerging shoots, and then slice the bottoms off plastic bottles and use these as cloches for the young plants as they get larger. Leafy vegetables prone to slug and snail attack, such as lettuce, will benefit especially from this protection. Discard the lids as the plants need fresh air. You can also use specially designed plastic row covers available in many garden centers and catalogs.

planters

Yogurt cartons, glass jars, and the bottom halves of soda bottles are perfect containers for seedlings. Glass jars have the advantage of weight, which makes them less likely to blow over than lighter plastic items. Because it is impossible to make a hole in the bottom of a jar safely, be sure to half-fill it with gravel or small pebbles for drainage.

You and your children can decorate your homemade planters by painting them with a matte acrylic paint or by sticking on shells, twigs, or pieces of broken china.

homemade cobbles

Use empty yogurt cartons as molds to make your own cobbles. Simply mix up some concrete, then pour into the cartons. Allow to set, then tap out the finished cobble. Special powder dyes can be added to the concrete when it is being mixed to change its color.

Above
An earthenware pitcher makes a good resting place for a bird and is also a good place for bird food.

Left
A cluster of homemade cloches made from old plastic bottles work like mini-greenhouses.

dangers

The number of children who are seriously injured in gardens every year is staggering. There are many thousands of serious accidents; the number of minor accidents is unquantifiable, as few ever get reported. Most of these injuries would never have happened if a few simple precautions had been taken.

▶general dangers

Above
Attach chicken wire over potentially slippery areas such as wood and stone.

There are many dangers in a garden, but there are precautions you can take.

• First, be disciplined when you garden. Lock up all tools and chemicals. Accidents with gardening tools, both manual and electrical, account for many thousands of injuries to children every year. Garden chemicals can be very dangerous and include weedkillers, pesticides, fertilizers, fungicides, disinfectants, and gasoline.

• Don't store chemicals anywhere that gets very hot, such as a greenhouse, as they may give off poisonous fumes or even catch fire. Keep oil and gasoline in metal containers and, if possible, buy chemicals in containers that have had a bittering agent added. This makes them unpalatable if a child does manage to get them open. Don't store chemicals in old soda bottles.

• Keep children away from any area that has recently been treated with weedkiller, pesticide, or fertilizer—even if the label says it is child-safe.

• Watch out for uneven surfaces that could trip a child or elderly person. Maintain all paths and steps, replacing broken paving slabs, steps, and loose stones.

• Prevent paths, steps, and patios from becoming slippery by removing overhanging branches. These encourage moss and algae to grow in their shade. Scrub off any algae and moss with hot soapy water or spray it with a high-pressure water jet attached to your garden hose. This is preferable to using chemical cleaners that may damage the hard surface over time. Sprinkling sharp sand over problem areas helps to provide grip and rub off algae. Wooden steps become slippery when wet, so cover them with chicken wire. Occasional use of a stiff brush prevents green slime from coating timber surfaces such as old railroad ties.

• Look out for protruding stems or branches that may scratch or cause eye injuries beside paths. Buy rubber caps for all wire plant supports.

• Your garden should never include unprotected sharp drops. Drops from a patio are especially dangerous, because running or cycling children can go over the edge. Situate greenhouses carefully, where children are safe from the danger of broken glass and the greenhouse is safe from flying balls.

• Never place play equipment near a greenhouse, railings, or clothesline.

• All gates should be fitted with childproof locks, and it's best to avoid fences with horizontal rails, because children can climb them. Be as prompt as possible in mending holes in hedges and fences, because children can squeeze through the smallest gaps.

▶burning garbage

Children find fire irresistible. Whether there is a small fire in a grill or a blazing bonfire, you can be certain that the smell of smoke and the glow and crackle of flames will attract them as surely as honey attracts bees.

Autumn is the best time for bonfires. Choose a windless day, so the fire is easy to control and you won't have to dodge the smoke as it constantly changes direction. Before you light the fire, check for any small mammals, such as woodchucks, that may have crawled into the pile to find shelter or hibernate. In the spring, make sure

The first rule is never to leave a fire untended in the garden, even if it is only a barbecue. Bonfires should be built away from sheds, fences, plants, and overhanging branches. Consider your neighbors and don't position a bonfire so that the smoke is likely to blow toward their houses or gardens.

Keep your bonfire material dry, so that it will burn quickly without producing clouds of choking smoke. You can cover the pile with a sheet of plastic or tarpaulin until you are ready to burn.

there are no birds' nests being built. Have a few buckets of water nearby in case of emergency. Try not to breathe in smoke, because some plants give off poisonous fumes. Be wary of stones or bits of glass, which may explode in the heat.

Instead of banning children from the garden when you have a bonfire, give them small tasks to perform, such as scouring the garden for waste material to burn or being on fire bucket duty. They will be kept busy, have lots of fun, and will feel involved so they will be far less likely to get into trouble.

▶water safety

Drowning in ponds and paddling pools accounts for the highest number of children's deaths in the garden. It is a terrifying fact that babies and small children can drown in as little as 2 inches (5 cm) of water.

Below
Place a strong fence around an existing pool to prevent danger to young children.

Older children and adults automatically hold their breath when their heads go under water, but small children and babies do exactly the opposite and take a deep breath in order to scream. Instead of getting lungfuls of air, they get lungfuls of water, and so they drown.

Be aware that if you have water in your garden it is a potentially fatal hazard. Some water features, such as small ponds and pools, can be filled in, eliminating the risk. Since this is not practical or even possible for large ponds, swimming pools, or streams, you must take precautions to reduce the danger from these features.

Once drained, a shallow pond may be turned into a sunken herb garden or sandpit. It will need a lid to prevent it from being flooded by rain. Larger ponds make excellent play areas once they are drained and filled with bark, wood chips, or sand.

If you do not want to drain your pool, cover it with rigid wire mesh. There are many brands on the market that are strong enough to take the weight of a child. Many are colored green to be unobtrusive, and large aquatic plants can grow through the holes in the mesh.

Swimming pools should be fitted with strong, child-proof covers and should be fenced off. Put a child-proof lock on the gate and never leave children unsupervised in the pool, even if they are able to swim. Don't allow unsupervised play in a paddling pool either, and when the children have finished playing, empty it and turn it upside down to prevent it from filling up with rainwater.

Gardens in a riverside setting are extremely desirable, but pose obvious risks to children. The only solution is to erect a strong fence. This need not be an eyesore, as you can disguise it by growing shrubs and flowers in front of it or training climbers along it. In this way, it becomes an attractive feature until the children are old enough for it to be taken down.

▶plant pests and diseases

Pests and diseases kill plants and need to be kept at bay. A discussion of pest and disease control logically falls into two parts: prevention and cure.

prevention

First, buy only the choicest plant specimens. Choose the healthiest, most vigorous-looking plants. Check that their roots are not pot-bound and that the plant is not dried out or already harboring a pest or disease. You can often tell if a plant has been in its container too long, because there is moss growing on the surface of the compost. Also check to be sure that you are not inadvertently buying some weeds along with your plant—the last thing anyone wants to do is to introduce yet another problem into the garden. Certain plants have been cross-bred with disease-resistant varieties. Seek these out wherever possible, because it will save a lot of trouble later on, especially if you are growing roses.

Follow recommendations as to planting position and conditions exactly, because if you place a plant in an unsuitable position, it will not thrive, no matter how healthy it is initially, or however much care and attention you lavish on it.

Practice good husbandry. Clear away weeds and debris that could provide hiding places for pests or act as a breeding ground for disease. Remove any dead, damaged, or diseased parts of plants, and always burn such material. Clean out the greenhouse regularly and be meticulous about cleaning and disinfecting your tools, especially hand pruners, shears, and pots, to prevent the spread of infection.

Erect barriers to deter pests. For example, net vegetables and grow soft fruit in a simple cage to keep the birds away. Protect fruit trees from pests by putting a grease band around the trunk in winter.

Spread gravel, prickly holly leaves, broken eggshells, or soot around the base of vulnerable plants, or, if they are grown in containers, paint pest-control glue around the rims. Slugs and snails do not like to cross such protective barriers, and gravel has the added advantage of acting as an excellent mulch

cure

There are many ways to control pests and diseases. However, remember that the safest way is the organic way.

manual pest removal

The most basic method of pest control can be tedious work, but it is also extremely satisfying—some even say addictive. After picking off pests, such as caterpillars, by

115

Above

A ladybug is one predator you should try to keep in your garden. Ladybugs are not only pretty, they also eat unwanted pests.

hand (if you are squeamish, wear thin gloves for this operation), don't just throw them away in a corner of the garden, as they'll simply return. They must be destroyed, for effective control. You will need to repeat the procedure at intervals of one or two weeks, until there are no signs of further infestation.

One way to deal with slugs and snails involves going out with a flashlight and a bucket of soapy water at night, picking off the slugs and snails, then dropping them in the bucket. This, however, is not a job for the faint-hearted. If you want to give slugs and snails a happy death, place bowls of beer on the ground among your flower beds.

Sticky insect traps have been used in greenhouses for a hundred years or so, and they still work well today. Position the traps close to the plants under attack and brush the plants to encourage the insects to leave them.

Set an earwig trap by filling a flower pot with straw or crumpled newspaper, then placing it upside down on a stick in your flower bed. Check it daily, and remove and destroy any earwigs you find.

You can wash aphids off plants with repeated sprayings of soapy water (make sure you wash the undersides of leaves where aphids congregate), but remember that birds, syrphidflies, and ladybugs love to eat them. In fact, one ladybug can dispose of 500 aphid larva and 5,000 adults during its lifetime.

companion planting

Certain plants, especially vegetables, benefit from companion planting, which is the growing of one plant beside another specifically to deter pests, distract them from the main plant, or attract their predators. Strong-smelling herbs, such as mint, are excellent in this role.

French marigolds (*Tagetes patula*) attract syrphid flies, which love to eat aphids, so it makes sense to grow them beside any vegetable that is susceptible to aphid attack.

Rosemary and lavender can be dried and used as a deterrent to stop moths from attacking linen and clothes; grown in the garden, these herbs protect plants from caterpillar attack. Moths also hate the strong smell of wormwood (*Artemesia absinthium*), which can be grown as a companion plant or made into an infusion to spray plants in need of protection.

Horsetail (*Equisetum arvense*) is an herb that works as a natural fungicide. It is effective against blackspot and mildew on roses.

natural predators

Avoid the use of chemical controls by encouraging beneficial predators. Learn to distinguish the goodies from the baddies. For example, centipedes are good, millipedes are bad; carnivorous beetles are good, herbivorous beetles are bad. Once you have identified friends and foes, you can encourage beneficial predators by avoiding chemicals and creating a habitat that your insect and animal helpers will enjoy (see page 78).

Insect-eating birds, such as blue tits, are welcome, as are ladybugs. You can encourage natural predators by filling a box with hollow stems from dead herbaceous plants and placing it high up in a tree or on a wall, where they can hibernate. You also want

Right
Small insects roll up
when threatened. They
are not harmful to
children unless a child
attempts to eat one.

Right
Small insects roll up
when threatened. They
are not harmful to
children unless a child
attempts to eat one.

plenty of spiders, syrphidflies, lacewing larvae, ladybugs, centipedes, carnivorous
beetles, bats, owls, frogs, and toads—all of
which eat insect pests at an amazing rate.

biological control

This is a relatively new and expensive
method of pest control, but one that can be
extremely effective. It involves the intro-
duction of microscopic parasitic insects
that will feed off the pest and ultimately kill
it. Examples are *Phytoseiulus*, which tar-
gets red spider mites, and *Encarsia formosa*,
a parasitic wasp that attacks whitefly. Such
controls tend to work best in enclosed areas
such as greenhouses and conservatories. If a
plant has been sprayed with any kind of
chemical, the eggs of the parasitic insect
may fail to hatch.

Many garden centers and mail order
companies supply biological controls, and
they are easy to apply. Beneficial nema-
todes, which are microscopic, parasitic
eelworms used to treat slugs and vine wee-
vils, are made up into a solution, then
watered into the soil around the affected
plants. It is, however, important to follow
the supplier's instructions as to application
times. If you release them when it is too
cold, they will die. In any event, they will
die soon after their victims are destroyed,
when there will be nothing for them to feed
on, so you will need to replace them each
year or until the problem is eradicated.

chemical control

Chemicals should only be used as a last
resort. If there is no alternative, it is essential to use them responsibly and sparingly
so that you affect beneficial wildlife as little
as possible. For example, if you have tried
unsuccessfully to control snails and slugs
with other means and feel slug pellets are
the only remaining option, you should use
the following technique.

Make a slit down one side of a plastic
water bottle and bend the edges back.
Scatter pellets inside, and half bury the
bottle among the plants under attack. The
slugs and snails will crawl into the bottle,
eat the pellets, and die. Be sure that the
pesticides are out of the reach of small children, who may think the brightly colored
pellets are candy. Also, the pellets should
be kept away from the soil, so they cannot
contaminate it. The bodies of the slugs and
snails, full of pesticide, are contained in the
bottle and should be disposed of safely
where birds or other predators cannot
reach them and where the pesticide can be
kept out of the food chain.

When spraying chemicals, be sure that
all children and pets are kept well away
from the area—even if the label says the
chemicals will not harm them. To avoid
harming beneficial insects, spray on a gray,
windless day—they will be less active than
on a hot, sunny one. If you have pond fish,
make sure there is absolutely no spray drift
over the water, because fish are extremely
sensitive to chemicals.

Wear protective clothing, including goggles and gloves, and immediately wash
away any accidental splashes on bare skin
using lots of cold water.

Reserve separate watering cans and
spray guns solely for chemical use, and
label them so there is no risk of confusion.

Other pests that are easily treatable by
this method include whitefly, red spider
mite, leatherjackets, and scale insects.

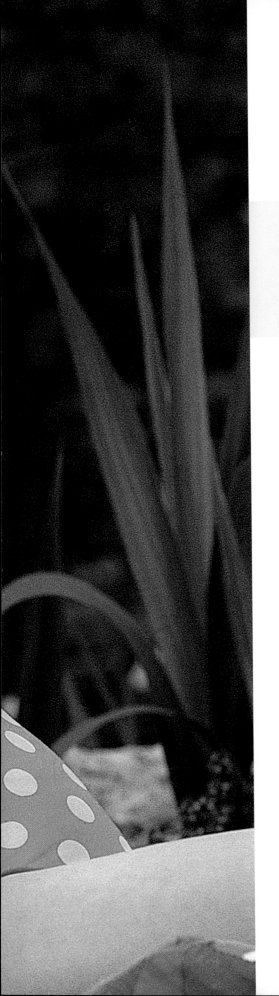

first aid and child care

In the event of an accident, the first thing to do is to stay calm. Your child is dependent on you for help, so you must be able to think calmly and clearly.

If a child is lying injured, call for an ambulance immediately. Do not hang up the telephone—even if you have had to rush back to the child before speaking to the operator. If you have not been able to give your full address and telephone number, but you have left the line open, the emergency operator can trace your address and send help. The operator can also give you instructions over the phone and help you stay calm.

Take your child to the hospital if he or she has fallen unconscious (even for a minute), is vomiting or drowsy (as there is a risk of concussion or shock), is bleeding from the ears, or has stopped breathing (even for a minute). Hospital treatment is also required if the child has a puncture wound or complains of severe pain.

Make sure that your family's tetanus shots are kept up-to-date, and it's a good idea to take a first aid course to give you greater confidence.

▶sun protection

The sun is a powerful life-giving force, without which no life on the planet would be possible. However, we now know that its power can be destructive. There are tens of thousands of new cases of skin cancer diagnosed every year, of which some are untreatable. In the United States, skin cancer is the biggest cause of death among women 25 to 30 years old. Treatment for skin cancer is unpleasant and leaves the patient with scars.

Below
The sun beating down on a child's head can cause sunstroke. It is important to ensure that a hat is worn at all times so that your child can enjoy time in the sun.

Even people who know how dangerous the sun can be find it difficult to absorb the idea that an attractive tan that makes you feel good is unhealthy. The skin turns brown in an attempt to protect itself from harmful rays, so a tan is a visible indication of damaged skin. Although it may look good in the short term, a tan soon fades, while the damage to the skin is permanent and can cause premature aging. Wrinkled, leathery skin is a legacy of excessive sun worship and inadequate precautions while young.

The effects of too much sun are also cumulative, and our children will not thank us in years to come if we don't protect them when they are at a vulnerable age. Babies and children, especially blonde, blue-eyed children from the northern hemisphere, have very delicate, sensitive skin that burns easily, even in sunlight too weak to affect grown-ups. It is unrealistic and unreasonable to expect them to stay in the shade when it is sunny, so it is vital to screen harmful rays.

Most children delight in wearing bright, colorful T-shirts, even in swimming or wading pools. There are also ultraviolet-proof all-in-one suits that look just like wet suits, so they have a cool cachet for even the most obstinate child.

Heads, faces, and backs of necks are especially vulnerable to the sun, so hats are important. For young children, French Legionnaire-style hats will protect the back of the neck and ears—areas often forgotten when sunscreens are applied. Older children may object to wearing hats. Girls may be persuaded if they are allowed to choose their own creation, but boys can be more difficult. A baseball cap in the colors of a favorite sports team, or a personalized cap may be the answer. The only

Right
Encourage your
children to apply
sunscreen and
encourage them
to rest in the shade.

disadvantage of baseball caps is that they don't cover the ears or neck, unless they're worn backward, in which case they don't cover the face. Don't forget the sunscreen, even when wearing a hat.

Choose a sunscreen with a factor 20 or above, apply it generously an hour before the child goes out, then every hour or so while the child is in the sun and especially after swimming. Try to avoid being in full sun during the hottest part of the day, and have lunch in the shade. If swimming is going to be the afternoon activity, make sure that lunch is fully digested before your child takes the plunge.

Harmful rays penetrate clouds and even burn when the sky is overcast. Water intensifies rays, so if you have a swimming or wading pool, apply extra sunscreen.

Never leave a baby sleeping in the sun. Always use a sunshade and check the baby frequently, because shady spots move as the sun moves.

If your child gets burned, gently cool the red areas with cold water from the faucet and apply calamine lotion or an after-sun

lotion to soothe the skin. Bring the child indoors, so that they can rest and recover out of the sun. Take the child to the doctor if the skin blisters over a wide area, or if the child develops a fever—a symptom of sunstroke.

Make sure your child has plenty to drink on a sunny day so that they keep cool and hydrated.

Below
Remember to reapply
sunscreen throughout
the day.

▶minor injuries

While minor sunburn, stings, bites, cuts, grazes, thorns, and splinters can be treated at home, more serious injuries require hospital attention. The first aid techniques described in this chapter are only emergency measures. If you have any question about the seriousness of your child's injury, call your local hospital or doctor's office and explain the situation.

Below
Knee and elbow pads and helmets will help protect against any nasty falls from bicycles, skateboards, and rollerblades.

cuts and grazes

Most children go through a stage when they always seem to be falling down and cutting or grazing themselves. This is when a well-stocked first aid box is invaluable. Knees and elbows take the most punishment. You can take preventive action by persuading your child to wear elbow and knee protectors when skating or cycling and sturdy pants when climbing.

Cuts and grazes can usually be treated at home. Common sense should tell you if a child needs medical attention, where for example the cut is especially large or deep, something is embedded in it, or it is too dirty to clean easily.

Clean cuts or grazes with cold running water, cotton balls soaked in warm water, or antiseptic wipes. Once it is thoroughly clean, a graze can be left uncovered to heal, whereas cuts should be protected and kept clean with a bandage or dressing. Change this every day until the cut has healed. Check for any signs of infection such as inflammation, soreness, or tenderness in the area of the cut.

If the cut is still bleeding after five minutes, make a pad out of a piece of clean fabric, such as a handkerchief, and press it against the wound for a few minutes. If possible, raise the limb with the cut above the level of the child's heart to stop the bleeding. Never use a tourniquet.

thorns and splinters

Children act as magnets for all sorts of thorns and splinters, which is compounded by their often stubborn refusal to wear shoes in the garden.

Holly, mahonia, pyracantha, and berberis are just a few of a long list of shrubs and plants with spikes and thorns that can be found in most gardens. It is inevitable that your child will manage to get a thorn or splinter embedded in his or her hand or foot at some point—often, during the summer months—so it is best to be prepared.

A small thorn or splinter may not hurt and, if left alone, may pop out of its own accord, often in a warm bath. However, a large thorn or splinter or anything embedded in the heel or the fingertips is bound to be painful and will need to be removed. The hardest part of the process will probably be keeping the child still while you're doing it. Try to get them interested in what you are doing, or tell them a story to distract and calm them.

If you can see the tip of the splinter, use a pair of tweezers that you have sterilized and gently pull it out. Pull it out straight to avoid breaking it, then wash the skin thoroughly and apply a drop of antiseptic.

If the tip of the splinter is just below the skin, you will need to sterilize a needle and use it to break the skin above the embedded tip of the splinter. Once the tip is revealed, use the needle point to lift it up enough to grasp it with the sterilized tweezers and pull it out. Again, clean the area and apply antiseptic.

Slivers of glass or metal and large splinters need medical attention. Watch out for signs of infection such as swelling, reddening, or undue tenderness.

bites, stings, and allergic reactions

The majority of bites and stings children are likely to suffer will only be minor, and although they may be painful they will not be dangerous. However, there is always a possibility that a child will develop an allergic reaction to a sting, which could bring on a convulsion or even anaphylactic shock. This is a life-threatening condition, and you must get the child to hospital immediately.

Bites and stings from spiders, snakes, or scorpions are very dangerous and require urgent hospital treatment. Even if the child appears to show no ill-effects, symptoms may develop later.

It may not be possible to identify the source of the wound, but if you can identify or describe the creature responsible, it will help the doctor to provide the right antidote. The first thing to do is to keep the child calm. Sit the child down, keeping the wound lower than the child's heart if possible. This slows down the spread of the poison. Don't attempt to suck the poison out, but wash around the area and then take the child straight to the hospital. If the child slips into unconsciousness, check his or her breathing and begin artificial respiration if it has stopped. If the child is still breathing, place him or her in the recovery position and call an ambulance.

Treatment for minor stings is straight forward. In the case of a bee sting, the stinger will have been left embedded in the skin and should be removed carefully. Wasps remove their stingers and may therefore sting more than once. Place a clean cloth soaked in very cold water over the wound. The skin around it will soon swell, becoming itchy and red, so soothe it with some calamine lotion, then apply some antihistamine ointment. Occasionally, children are stung in the mouth, in which case a cold drink will help reduce the swelling. Sucking an ice cube may also help, but do not give one to a child under two because of the danger of choking.

Certain plants can trigger an allergic reaction in children (see page 97).

Above
Overhanging branches can be dangerous, so keep them trimmed.

Above
Look out for thorns, although once pricked by thorns, most children will stay away!

Above
Berries may look tempting to a child, but many will cause an upset stomach.

▶emergency action

Below
It is vital that every parent knows how to place someone in the recovery position. It makes recovery from trauma easier and is more comfortable for the patient.

However careful you are, accidents will happen because children are so active and unpredictable. If there is a bad accident and a child is unconscious, there are a few basic emergency rules that can mean the difference between life and death.

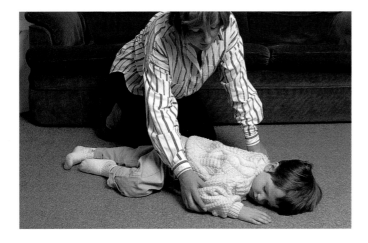

On finding a child unconscious, your first reaction will probably be to rush right over to help, but you should take a second to assess the situation, in case there is some danger that might incapacitate you, too, or hinder your rescue attempt.

Now check the child's responses. Talk to the child, call the child's name, tap the soles of the child's feet, but never shake the child, as this could worsen any injury.

If there is no response, the child is unconscious and you must check his or her breathing immediately, because any delay in getting air into the child's lungs could result in brain damage. Place your head sidewise,

so that you have one ear by the child's mouth and nose and are looking toward the child's chest. In this position, you can listen for breathing, feel breath against your cheek, and see whether the chest is moving. Allow ten seconds for this.

If you cannot detect any breathing, you must give mouth-to-mouth resuscitation (also known as artificial respiration or mouth-to-mouth ventilation).

First, make sure that nothing is blocking the child's airway. Open the mouth and, using your finger, gently clear away any obvious obstruction that may be preventing the child from breathing, such as vomit or dirt. Do this very carefully to avoid pushing the obstruction farther down the child's throat. Next, roll the child onto his or her back and tilt the head back by lifting the chin with one hand and gently pressing the forehead with your other hand. Open the child's mouth. This movement will lift the tongue away from the back of the throat.

mouth-to-mouth resuscitation

Resuscitation techniques for babies and children under two are different from techniques for older children.

Tilt the baby's or toddler's head back and place one hand on the forehead and the other under the back of the neck to support the head in the correct position. Now breathe into the mouth and nose simultaneously.

For an older child, pinch the child's nostrils together with one hand, place your other hand on the chin to hold the mouth open, then put your mouth completely over the child's mouth and blow gently until you see the chest rise. Stop blowing and allow the chest to fall, then repeat the action four times. If after five breaths the child is still not breathing, check the circulation by listening for a heartbeat or feeling for a pulse. The carotid pulse in the neck is the easiest to find by placing two fingers in the hollows on either side of the voice box. Allow ten seconds to detect the pulse.

If there is no pulse, you must give chest compressions (also known as heart massage) in addition to mouth-to-mouth resuscitation. Ask someone to help if available.

chest compressions

Place the heel of your hand just above the "v" where the ribs meet the breastbone and press down to a third of the depth of the chest five times, taking five seconds to complete the cycle. For babies and children under two, use only two fingers and exert less pressure to avoid damaging the ribs.

Alternate the mouth-to-mouth resuscitation and chest compressions at a rate of one breath to five compressions. If the child has a pulse but is not breathing, administer ten breaths a minute, then check the pulse for ten seconds. Once the heart starts beating stop the compressions, but continue artificial respiration until the child or baby starts breathing unaided.

An easy way to remember the routine is to think of it as **ABC**. **A** is for airways, **B** is for breathing, **C** is for circulation. All must be checked and assisted, in that order.

recovery position

Once the child has a pulse and is able to breathe, place the child in the recovery position. If someone is left lying on their back while unconscious, there is a danger that they may choke on their tongue or vomit. The recovery position prevents the tongue from obstructing the passage of air and should be used unless you think the child may have a broken back or neck.

Roll the child gently onto his or her side, then straighten the lower leg, bend the top leg, stretch out the lower arm, and finally, bend the top arm and rest the head on it. This will prevent the child from rolling onto his or her back.

shock and concussion

After a bad accident a child may suffer shock. This is potentially a life-threatening state of collapse that must be taken seriously. It is the body's way of coping with an injury by drawing blood away from the extremities toward the vital organs.

The symptoms of shock include the following: The child may seem drowsy or confused, breathing may become shallow and fast, the skin may become cold, pale, and sweaty, the skin under the fingernails or inside the lips may take on a gray-blue tinge, and the child may even lose consciousness altogether.

Call an ambulance, then place the child on his or her back. As long as you are sure there is no head or leg injury, raise the legs 8 inches (20 cm) to help more blood go to the head. Place a cushion or pillow beneath the feet to keep them elevated, and cover the child with a blanket. Do not, however, allow the child to get too hot.

Don't give the child anything to drink, although you may use a damp cloth to moisten his or her lips. Keep a close watch on the child's breathing, and if it stops, start mouth-to-mouth resuscitation at once.

Concussion occurs when the brain is shaken or when there is bleeding within the skull and is caused by a serious blow to the head. The symptoms of concussion may be delayed by up to 24 hours and can be extremely varied.

The baby or child may become unconscious or the signs may be negligible. The child may behave a bit oddly, develop an aversion to bright light or a severe headache, or be unusually drowsy. Sometimes the symptoms include unusual crying, noisy breathing or snoring, vomiting, or a discharge from the nose or ear.

If the baby or child has had a blow to the head, watch carefully for signs of concussion and, if any appear, seek emergency help immediately.

Index

Photo Credits